That Your Joy May Be Full

by Florence M. Taylor

author of *You Don't Have to Be Old When You Grow*

BRIDGE PUBLISHING, INC.
Publishers of:
LOGOS • HAVEN • OPEN SCROLL

Other books by Florence M. Taylor:
> *You Don't Have to Be Old When You Grow Old*
> *Thou Art My God*
> *As for Me and My Family: The Christian Family—A Redemptive Fellowship*
> *In the Morning, Bread: Devotions for a New Day*
> *The Bridled Tongue: Bible Words About Words*

THAT YOUR JOY MAY BE FULL
Copyright © by Bridge Publishing, Inc.
All rights reserved
Printed in the United States of America
Library of Congress Catalog Card Number: 82-84718
International Standard Book Number: 0-88270-547-4
Bridge Publishing, Inc., South Plainfield, New Jersey 07080

Contents

Part I: Joy Is Biblical
1. What Is Joy? 5
2. Joy in the Old Testament 11
3. Joy in the New Testament 23
4. Jesus' Own Words About Joy 35
5. Joy in the Acts of the Apostles 41

Part II: Living With Joy: The Christian's Responsibility
6. Jesus' Directives:
   The "Good and Satisfying Things" 51
7. Jesus' Directives (Concluded) 57
8. Living With Joy:
   Our Responsibility as Christians 69
9. Living With Joy:
   Our Responsibility as Christians (Continued) 75

Part III: Living With Joy Through Various Afflictions
10. Bible Words About Affliction 83
11. Living With Joy Through Life's "Afflictions" 91
12. Some Common Obstacles To Living With Joy ... 103
13. Some Common Obstacles To Living With Joy
    (Continued) 109
14. Some Common Obstacles To Living With Joy
    (Continued) 117
15. Some Common Obstacles To Living With Joy
    (Concluded) 127
16. Living With Joy Through the Experience
    of "Aloneness" 137
17. Living With Joy Through the Experience
    of Bereavement 149

Part IV: "Our Father": Prayers of Faith and Joy
18. "Lord, Teach Us to Pray" 159

    Appendix A: A Special Word for Parents 177
    Appendix B: "God Calling" 183

Biblical Quotations

The sources of the biblical quotations throughout the book are identified as follows:

GNB—GOOD NEWS BIBLE. TODAY'S ENGLISH VERSION
    American Bible Society
    New York, 1976

JBP—THE NEW TESTAMENT IN MODERN ENGLISH
    Translated by J.B. Phillips
    The Macmillian Company, New York, 1963

KJV—THE HOLY BIBLE, OLD AND NEW TESTAMENTS IN THE KING JAMES VERSION
    Thomas Nelson, Inc.
    Nashville, Tenn.

TLB—THE LIVING BIBLE, PARAPHRASED
    Tyndale House Publishers, 1971
    Wheaton, Ill 60187

NAS—NEW AMERICAN STANDARD BIBLE
    Foundation Press, 1960-1972
    Box 6439, Anaheim, Cal. 92806

NBY—THE NEW BERKLEY VERSION IN MODERN ENGLISH
    Gerrit Verkuyl, Editor-in-chief
    Zondervan Publishing House
    Grand Rapids, Michigan

NEB—THE NEW ENGLISH BIBLE. NEW TESTAMENT
    Oxford University Press
    Cambridge University Press
    1961

To The Reader

In his book, *Sermons on the Psalms,* Harold Bosley records the following incident:

> In a black church on the South Side during my student days at the University of Chicago, a panel of speakers consisting of Charles Gilkey of the University Chapel and Clarence Darrow, and two other speakers were addressing a church packed with people, mostly black. The depression was at its worst at that time; money and jobs were scarce, and the morale of everyone was on the floor. Clarence Darrow took advantage of that fact to point out the plight of the black people. He summed up their woes, concluding, "And yet you sing! No one can sing like you do! What do you have to sing about?"
>
> Quick as a flash, a lady in the congregation shouted, "We've got Jesus to sing about!"
>
> For once Darrow was stopped dead in his tracks. He was face to face with one who had faith in the fact that "weeping may endure for a night but joy cometh in the morning."

"We've got Jesus to sing about!" This book has been compiled in the firm conviction that in the birth of Jesus, in His life, death and resurrection, God has provided us with unlimited supplies of everything we need to live joyous, triumphant lives, no matter what the circumstances of those lives may be.

It has been compiled also because more and more in these later years of my life, the conviction has been growing in my heart, that those of us who are claiming to be Christians (or are trying to be!) have an inescapable responsibility to live lives characterized by JOY.

It is my hope that as you read and reread these selections and meditate upon them, you may find the "joy of the Lord" becoming a greater reality in your daily living, and that you will grow in your ability to "rejoice in the Lord alway" (Phil. 4:4).

And now, "May the Lord bless and protect you; may the Lord's face radiate with joy because of you; may he be gracious to you, show you his favor, and give you his peace" (Numbers 6:24-26 TLB).

Florence Taylor
Columbus, Ohio

Part I

Joy Is Biblical

Thy Holy Word

O gracious God, and most merciful Father, who hast vouchsafed us the rich and precious jewel of thy holy Word:

Assist us with the Spirit that it may be written in our hearts to our everlasting comfort, to reform us, according to thine own image, to build us up, to edify us . . . sanctifying and increasing in us all heavenly virtues.

Grant this, O heavenly Father, For Jesus Christ's sake. Amen.

—From the *Preface to the Geneva Bible*

1

What Is Joy?

It may seem superfluous to start off our consideration of Christian joy with definitions of joy; most of us have a clear idea of what joy means, both in its form as a noun, and in its verbal derivative, "Rejoice!" There are, however, some interesting insights to be gained from consulting the dictionary.[1]

1. *Joy: an "emotion."*
The first definition of *joy* is "the emotion caused by something good or satisfying."
"Something good or satisfying" is a term of great indefiniteness! It is capable of innumerable interpretations. What gives one person "joy" may be to another a "trial" or "tribulation."
Many people seek joy through the acquisition of material

possessions, but there is much that money cannot buy. Josh Billings once said: "Money will buy a pretty good dog; but it won't buy the wag of his tail."[2]

Wallace Viets has written:

> How many persons there are, who in their personal lives, seek for happiness and meaning through possessing things! We live in a time when more people have more things to use and enjoy than ever before in the history of mankind. Are we happier? Have we found meaning? Have the television sets, fast cars, automatic washers really freed us for relaxed and creative activity? I remember so well the childless couple who came to me for counsel in a former parish. Their income was at least twice the income on which I was raising four children. They were miserable, in spite of their Cadillac roadster and their second car, together with so much of what money could buy, for they had no purpose. Then there was the man who felt he was doing his duty to God by putting five dollars on the offering plate every Easter, but who, despite his belief that he could handle his own affairs, was spending twenty-five dollars for a half-hour with a psychiatrist every week, as his second marriage was going on the rocks.[3]

John Oxenham has written about "true Happiness":

Some have much and some have more,
Some are rich and some are poor.
Some have little, some have less,
Some have not a cent to bless
Their empty pockets, yet possess
True riches in true happiness.[4]

Some people seek joy through success in a chosen profession or vocation; still others seek it through indulging the physical cravings of their bodies. None of these will result in permanent joy. Christian joy alone is a quality of life independent of any outward circumstances.

2. *Joy: a by-product.*
The definition of by-product is a "secondary or incidental product."

> Many of the things we most desire can be attained only if we do not aim directly at them. They are, as it were, by-products of something else.
>
> Happiness is one of these things. If you go after it directly and of set purpose, you miss it entirely. You may, of course, have what you are pleased to call a good time, but that is quite a different thing and it does not last long.[5]

This aspect of joy has been widely recognized. Consider these lines of Gerald Massey's:

> Not by appointment do we meet Delight
> And Joy: they heed not our expectancy
> But round some corner in the streets of life
> They, on a sudden, clasp us with a smile.[6]

"Gladness Unsought." In his book, *The New Life*, Andrew Murray comments on this point:

> Understand this saying: "He that seeks gladness shall not find it; he that seeks the Lord and His will, shall find gladness unsought." He that seeks gladness as a thing of feeling ... will not find it. He that forgets himself to live in the Lord and His will shall be taught of himself to rejoice in the Lord. It is God, God Himself, who is the God of the gladness of our rejoicing. Seek God and you have gladness. You have then simply to take and enjoy it by faith.[7]

3. *Joy: a paradox.*
The dictionary defines *paradox* as "a statement or

proposition seemingly self-contradictory or absurd, but in reality expressing a possible truth."

The Beatitudes. In his article quoted above, T.M. Taylor has these additional comments:

> You cannot read the Gospels without seeing that Jesus did not tell men how to be good in the manner of the moralists of every age; He told them how to be happy. The Sermon on the Mount, for instance, contains among other things a series of recipes for happiness .... These are genuine paradoxes—they sound absurdly impossible, but how true they prove to be!

Gerald Kennedy comments on Jesus' use of paradox:

> ... Jesus announced great paradoxes. He tells us that if we want to find something we have to lose it, which is not logical, but is grandly true. He speaks of the joy of sacrifice and of the happiness of service. He tells about the divine surprises in life which come to those who choose his way. He never offered men ease, but he promised a strange, almost absurd kind of joy if we set our minds on seeking the Kingdom of God.[8]

It is interesting to read the Beatitudes as *The Living Bible* paraphrases them:

> Then he turned to his disciples and said, "What happiness there is for you who are poor, for the Kingdom of God is yours! What happiness there is for you who are now hungry, for you are going to be satisfied! What happiness there is for you who weep, for the time will come when you shall laugh with joy! What happiness it is when others hate you and exclude you and insult you and smear your name because you are mine! When that happens, rejoice! Yes, leap for joy! For you will have a great reward awaiting you in heaven. And you will be in good company—the ancient prophets were treated that way too! (Luke 6:20-23, TLB)

4. *Joy: a bonus*
Still another definition of *joy* is that it is a *bonus*. The dictionary defines *bonus* as "something given or paid over and above what is due . . . something extra or additional given freely." Christian joy surely fits that definition—it is a free gift from God, unearned and undeserved.

5. *Summary.*
Christian joy may be defined in all these ways:
- it is "an emotion caused by something good and satisfying";
- it is a "by-product," of certain fulfilled conditions;
- it is a "paradox"—a reality in the midst of sorrow, suffering, tragedy;
- it is a "bonus," bestowed on us by God himself, over and above anything we could possibly deserve.

Joseph Fort Newton comments:

No other of God's promises seems to be less appropriated than the promise of joy: ministers preach about it; a few rare souls truly possess it, and share it irresistibly and effortlessly with those around them.

[Christian] joy is not dependent upon material possessions nor outward circumstances. It is an inner glow—steady, warm, indestructible. You cannot will yourself to be joyous. You can only will yourself to be and to do those things which inevitably produce joy. It comes as a free gift unearned and even unsought, when certain conditions are fulfilled. When your relationship with God is "right," when you have accepted Jesus as your personal Lord and Savior, when you have invited the Holy Spirit to indwell you, so that "rivers of living water" are flowing out of your life into the world around you . . . then some day you will be "surprised by joy" and you will have taken possession of your rightful heritage as a Christian.[9]

2

Joy in the Old Testament

Since this book is about *Christian* joy it is clear that our search for understanding will lead us into the New Testament—our record of Jesus' life, death and resurrection, of His teachings and of His influence on His early followers.

Although this is the main source of our study there is a great deal of important relevant material in the Old Testament, those sacred writings of His people in which Jesus' mind and heart had been steeped in His childhood and young manhood.

1. *Joy in Creation.*
And so as we begin our consideration of biblical joy it is interesting to note that biblical joy appears very early in the Bible.

Long before Jesus came to give His "joy to the world" God had revealed to His chosen people that joy was an important part of His provision for them.

Alexander Miller sees evidence of this in the story of Creation:

> The primeval account of Adam and Eve in the plenitude of created and creative power, inhabiting "a garden filled with all manner of fruits" is a picture of such divine exhilaration in creation, as forces us, if we are asked to say summarily why God made the world, to affirm that He made it for fun! There is no purpose in it save the purpose of joy: the joy of the Maker in the world of His making, and the derivative and reciprocal joy of the world itself, and in Him who made it.[1]

Malcolm Smith also has something to say about the joy of the early Hebrews:

> To the believing Israelites, religion was not a dismal affair, but rejoicing in God with heart, mind and body.... The Hebrews saw all creation moving in joyous praise to the Creator. The hills danced and sang, the trees clapped their hands, and the whole earth and sky shouted in ecstasy at the sight of God's glory.[2]

2. *Declarations of Joy.*

The joy of the Lord is your strength. (Neh. 8:10, KJV)

My soul shall be joyful in the Lord: it shall rejoice in his salvation. (Ps. 35:9, KJV)

The Lord hath done great things for us; whereof we are glad. (Ps. 126:3, KJV)

This is the day which the Lord hath made; we will rejoice and be glad in it. (Ps. 118:24, KJV)

... God giveth to a man that is good in his sight wisdom, and knowledge, and joy .... (Eccles. 2:26a, KJV)

How blessed is the man who does not walk in the counsel
   of the wicked,
Nor stand in the path of sinners,
Nor sit in the seat of scoffers!
But his delight is in the law of the Lord,
And in His law he meditates day and night.
And he will be like a tree firmly planted by streams of
   water,
Which yields its fruit in its season,
And its leaf does not wither
And in whatever he does, he prospers. (Ps. 1:1-3, NAS)

Happy are all who perfectly follow the laws of God. Happy are all who search for God, and always do his will, rejecting compromise with evil, and walking only in his paths. (Ps. 119:1-3, TLB)

... He turned my sorrow into joy! He took away my clothes of mourning and gave me gay and festive garments to rejoice in so that I might sing glad praises to the Lord .... (Ps. 30:11-12, TLB)

... The eyes of the Lord are watching over those who fear him, who rely upon his steady love .... We depend upon the Lord alone to save us. Only he can help us; he protects us like a shield. No wonder we are happy in the Lord! For we are trusting him. We trust his holy name. (Ps. 33:18-21, TLB)

Praise the Lord! For all who fear God and trust in him are blessed beyond expression. Yes, happy is the man who delights in doing his commands. (Ps. 112:1, TLB)

3. *Directives: Be Joyful!*

Shout with joy before the Lord, O earth! Obey him gladly; come before him, singing with joy.

Try to realize what this means—the Lord is God! He made us—we are his people, the sheep of his pasture.

Go through his open gates with great thanksgiving;

enter his courts with praise. Give thanks to him and bless his name. For the Lord is always good. He is always loving and kind, and his faithfulness goes on and on to each succeeding generation. (Ps. 100, TLB)

Awake, awake; put on thy strength, O Zion; put on thy beautiful garments, O Jerusalem . . . .

How beautiful upon the mountains are the feet of him that bringeth good tidings, that publisheth peace; that bringeth good tidings of good, that publisheth salvation; that saith unto Zion, Thy God reigneth!

Break forth into joy, sing together . . . for the Lord hath comforted his people, he hath redeemed Jerusalem. (Isa. 52:1, 7, 9, KJV)

. . . Thou shalt rejoice in every good thing which the LORD thy God hath given unto thee, and unto thine house . . . . (Deut. 26:11, KJV)

Glory ye in his holy name: let the heart of them rejoice that seek the Lord.(1 Chron. 16:10, KJV)

Let the heavens be glad, and let the earth rejoice: and let men say among the nations, The LORD reigneth. (1 Chron. 16:31, KJV)

Let all those that seek thee rejoice and be glad in thee: let such as love thy salvation say continually, The LORD be magnified. (Ps. 40:16, KJV)

. . . Let the righteous be glad; let them rejoice before God: yea, let them exceedingly rejoice. (Ps. 68:3, KJV)

Rejoice in the LORD, ye righteous; and give thanks at the remembrance of his holiness. (Ps. 97:12, KJV)

The LORD reigneth; let the earth rejoice; let the multitude of isles be glad thereof. (Ps. 97:1, KJV)

What happiness for those whose guilt has been forgiven! What joys when sins are covered over! What relief for those who have confessed their sins and God has cleared their record . . . .

Many sorrows come to the wicked, but abiding love surrounds those who trust in the Lord. So rejoice in him, all those who are his, and shout for joy, all those who try to obey him. (Ps. 32:1-2, 10-11, TLB)

Oh, praise the Lord, for he has listened to my pleadings! He is my strength, my shield from every danger. I trusted in him, and he helped me. Joy rises in my heart until I burst out in songs of praise to him. (Ps. 28:6-7, TLB)

Sing a new song to the Lord! . . . Sing out his praises! Bless his name.

For the Lord is great beyond description, and greatly to be praised.

Let the heavens be glad, the earth rejoice; let the vastness of the roaring seas demonstrate his glory. (Ps. 96:1, 2, 4, 11, TLB)

Praise God forever! How he must rejoice in all his work! The earth trembles at his glance; the mountains burst into flame at his touch.

I will sing to the Lord as long as I live. I will praise God to my last breath! May he be pleased by all these thoughts about him, for he is the source of all my joy . . . . Hallelujah! (Ps. 104:31-34, TLB)

4. *Joy in Proverbs.*

. . . The Lord grants wisdom! His every word is a treasure of knowledge and understanding. He grants good sense to the godly—his saints. He is their shield, protecting them and guarding their pathway. He shows how to distinguish right from wrong, how to find the right decision every time. For wisdom and truth will enter the very center of your being, filling your life with joy. (Prov. 2:6-10, TLB)

The man who knows right from wrong and has good judgment and common sense is happier than the man who is immensely rich! For such wisdom is far more valuable than precious jewels. Nothing else compares with it. (Prov. 3:13-15, TLB)

Ill-gotten gain brings no lasting happiness; right living does. (Prov. 10:2, TLB)

When a man is gloomy, everything seems to go wrong; when he is cheerful, everything seems right! (Prov. 15:15, TLB)

God blesses those who obey him; happy the man who puts his trust in the Lord. (Prov. 16:20, TLB)

Reverence for God gives life, happiness, and protection from harm. (Prov. 19:23, TLB)

5. *A Joyous Occasion*—Selected Verses From 1 Chronicles 16, KJV.

When David prepared a tabernacle for the Lord and brought up the Ark and "set it in the midst of the tent that he had pitched," it was a time of great joy and celebration; for the Ark was the symbol of God's presence with His people. On that day David expressed his rejoicing in ever-living words:

Give thanks unto the LORD, call upon his name, make known his deeds among the people.

Sing unto him, sing psalms unto him, talk ye of all his wondrous works.

Glory ye in his holy name: let the heart of them rejoice that seek the LORD.

Seek the LORD and his strength, seek his face continually.

Remember his marvellous works that he hath done. . . . (8-12a)

Sing unto the LORD, all the earth . . .

For great is the LORD, and greatly to be praised . . . . (23a, 25a)

Glory and honour are his presence; strength and gladness are in his place.

Let the heavens be glad . . . and let men say among the nations, The LORD reigneth.

Let the sea roar, and the fulness thereof: let the fields rejoice, and all that is therein.

Then shall the trees of the wood sing out at the presence of the LORD . . . .

O give thanks unto the LORD; for he is good; for his mercy endureth forever . . . . (27, 31-34)

And all the people said, Amen . . . . (36)

6. *Prophecies of the Messiah and His Kingdom.*

From the first mention in the Bible of God's plan for the world, joy is promised to all people everywhere; the Hebrew nation was being formed for the purpose of "blessing"—making joyful—all mankind (see Gen. 12:1-3).

Halley's *Bible Handbook* contains a chapter entitled "Messianic Strain of the Old Testament—Foreshadows and Predictions of the Coming Messiah," (pp. 387-401). The chapter is too long to be included here. The concluding "Summary" however, in somewhat shortened form, is given below, followed by some selected biblical passages to which reference has been made.

> Near the beginning of the Old Testament it is stated that the Hebrew Nation was being founded for the purpose of blessing All Nations. Then there begins to loom the figure of ONE PERSON through whom the nation will accomplish its mission . . . .
>
> Over and over He is spoken of as a King, to arise in David's Family, to be called The Branch, The Prince, The Anointed One, God's First-born, Wonderful, Mighty God, Everlasting Father, the Prince of Peace.
>
> The exact time of His Coming was Foretold, He was to be born of a Virgin. At Bethlehem. Part of His Childhood to be spent in Egypt. He would be brought up at Nazareth.

He would be introduced to His nation by an Elijah-like fore-runner. Galilee to be the scene of His ministry. He would work miracles of healing. And speak in parables. Be rejected by leaders of His Own Nation. Be a smitten shepherd, a Sufferer, a Man of Sorrows. He would enter Jerusalem riding on a colt. He would be betrayed by a Friend, for thirty pieces of silver to be spent for a potter's field. He would be led as a lamb to the slaughter.

He would die with the wicked, opening a Fountain for sin, Removing Sin in One Day. Even His Dying Words Foretold. He would be given gall and vinegar in His agony. His hands and feet would be pierced. Not a bone to be broken. Lots to be cast for His Garments. To be buried with the rich. To be in the tomb Three Days. To rise from the Dead and ascend to Heaven at God's Right Hand.

It was foretold that . . . He would offer a New Covenant to mankind . . . . That He would introduce an Era of the Holy Spirit, That His Kingdom would include Gentiles, and be universal and endless.

This Prewritten Story of Jesus, recorded centuries before He came, is as Astonishing in Detail that it reads like an Eye-witness account of His life and work . . . .

And how can this amazing Composite of Jesus' life and Work put together by different writers of different Centuries, Ages before Jesus Came, be explained on any other basis than that ONE SUPERHUMAN MIND supervised the writing? The Miracles of the Ages!

(1)
The Coming Kingdom

"And there shall come forth a root out of the stem of Jesse, and a Branch shall grow out of his roots:

"And the spirit of the LORD shall rest upon him, the spirit of wisdom and understanding, the spirit of counsel and might, the spirit of knowledge and of the fear of the LORD;

"And shall make him of quick understanding in the fear of the Lord: and he shall not judge after the sight of his eyes, neither reprove after the hearing of his ears:

"But with righteousness shall he judge the poor, and reprove with equity for the meek of the earth: and he shall smite the earth with the rod of his mouth, and with the breath of his lips shall he slay the wicked.

"And righteousness shall be the girdle of his loins, and faithfulness the girdle of his reins.

"The wolf also shall dwell with the lamb, and the leopard shall lie down with the kid; and the calf and the young lion and the fatling together; and a little child shall lead them . . . . They shall not hurt nor destroy in all my holy mountain: for the earth shall be full of the knowledge of the Lord, as the waters cover the sea" (Isa. 11:1-6, 9 KJV).

(2)
The Holy Highway

"Search the Book of the Lord and see all that he will do; not one detail will he miss . . . for the Lord has said it, and his Spirit will make it all come true.

"Even the wilderness and desert will rejoice in those days; the desert will blossom with flowers. Yes, there will be an abundance of flowers and singing and joy! The deserts will become as green as the Lebanon mountains . . . for the Lord will display his glory there . . . .

"With this news bring cheer to all discouraged ones. . . . Tell them, 'Be strong, fear not, for your God is coming . . . to save you.' And when he comes, he will open the eyes of the blind, and unstop the ears of the deaf. The lame man will leap up like a deer, and those who could not speak will shout and sing! Springs will burst forth in the wilderness, and streams in the desert. The parched ground will become a pool, with springs of water in a thirsty land....

"And a main road will go through that once-deserted land: it will be named 'The Holy Highway.' No evil-hearted men may walk upon it. God will walk there with you ... only the redeemed will travel there. These, the ransomed of the Lord, will go home along that road to Zion, singing the songs of everlasting joy. For them all sorrow and all sighing will be gone forever; only joy and gladness will be there" (Isa. 34:16; 35:1-10, TLB).

(3)
In the Last Days

(A Magnificent Prevision of
the Joy of the Kingdom of God on Earth)

"But in the last days it shall come to pass, that the mountain of the house of the LORD shall be established in the top of the mountains, and it shall be exalted above the hills; and people shall flow into it.

"And many nations shall come, and say, Come, and let us go up to the mountain of the Lord, and to the house of the God of Jacob; and he will teach us of his ways, and we will walk in his paths: for the law shall go forth of Zion, and the word of the Lord from Jerusalem.

"And he shall judge among many people, and rebuke strong nations afar off; and they shall beat their swords into plowshares, and their spears into pruninghooks: nation shall not lift up a sword against nation, neither shall they learn war any more.

"But they shall sit every man under his vine and under his fig tree; and none shall make them afraid: for the mouth of the LORD of hosts hath spoken it" (Mic. 4:1-4, KJV).

(4)
The Oil of Joy

"The spirit of the Lord God is upon me; because the LORD hath anointed me to preach good tidings unto the meek; he hath sent me to bind up the brokenhearted, to proclaim liberty to the captives, and the opening of the prison to them that are bound ... to comfort all that mourn ... to give unto them beauty for ashes, the oil of joy for mourning, the garment of praise for the spirit of heaviness ...." (Isa. 61:1-3, KJV).

(In sharp contrast to these joyful prophecies is the following selection from Isaiah 53 foreshadowing the sufferings of Christ. How utterly amazing this is, when we consider that it was written about 700 years before the birth of Jesus!)

"Who hath believed our report? and to whom is the arm of the Lord revealed?

"For he shall grow up before him as a tender plant, and as a root out of dry ground: he hath no form nor comeliness; and when we shall see him, there is no beauty that we should desire him.

"He is despised and rejected of men; a man of sorrows, and acquainted with grief: and we hid as it were our faces from him; he was despised, and we esteemed him not.

"Surely he hath borne our griefs, and carried our sorrows: yet we did esteem him stricken, smitten of God, and afflicted.

"But he was wounded for our transgressions, he was bruised for our iniquities: the chastisement of our peace was upon him; and with his stripes we are healed" (Isa. 53:1-5, KJV).

7. Jehovah: "I AM."

The joy revealed in the Old Testament grew out of their faith and belief in the one God—Jehovah. This name, given to God most frequently, means "I Am." In a little book called *We Would See Jesus*, the authors give the following interpretation of "I Am":

"I am" is an incomplete sentence. It has no object. I am—what? What is our wonder when we discover as we continue with our Bibles, that He is saying, "I AM whatever my people need," and that the sentence is only left blank that man may bring his many and various needs, as they arise, to complete it! . . .

The name Jehovah is really like a blank check. Your faith can fill in what He is to be to you—just what you need as each need arises. It is not you, moreover, who are beseeching Him for this privilege, but He is pressing it upon you. He is asking you to ask. "Hitherto have ye asked nothing in My name: ask, and ye shall receive, that your joy may be full" (John 16:24). Just as water is ever seeking the lowest depths in order to fill them, so is Jehovah ever seeking out man's need in order to satisfy it. Where there is need, there is God. Where there is sorrow, misery, unhappiness, suffering, confusion, folly, oppression, there is the I AM, yearning to turn man's sorrow into bliss, whenever man will let Him. It is not, therefore, the hungry seeking for bread, but the Bread seeking the hungry: not the sad seeking for joy, but rather Joy seeking the sad; not emptiness seeking fulness, but rather Fulness seeking emptiness. And it is not merely that He supplies our need, but He becomes Himself the fulfillment of our need. He is ever "I AM that which my people need."

3

Joy in the New Testament

The Joy of Christ.
We turn now from our consideration of "Joy in the Old Testament" to seek a deeper understanding of *Christian* joy by studying the pages of the New Testament. Obviously *Christian joy* cannot be understood apart from *Christ.*

There are of course other kinds of happiness that are unrelated to Jesus—worldly pleasures that come from worldly experiences, pleasure in the acquisition of worldly possessions, pleasure in worldly success, in the achievement of excellence in many areas of endeavor (in sports, in vocations, in educational pursuits, in overcoming handicaps, in receiving honors for professional achievement). The list is long and varied. But all of these fail to satisfy the deepest yearnings of our hearts.

Only in Christian joy, the joy of Christ himself, do we find a joy and peace completely independent of outward circumstances, the "joy unspeakable and full of glory" (1 Pet. 1:8).

"To Enjoy Him Forever."
   The divines who in the seventeenth century produced

the Westminster Confession answered the question, "What is the chief end of man?" with the words, "Man's chief end is to glorify God, and *to enjoy Him forever*"(Page 10).

This then is the purpose of life . . . to see God, and to allow Him to bring us . . . to the . . . relationship of submission to Himself . . . . Our highest good is achieved only in submitting. It has been said that there is a God-shaped blank in every man's heart. It is also true that there is a man-shaped blank in God's heart. It is because of the latter that God yearns so much for us and pursues us so relentlessly, and it is because of the former that mere earthly things . . . will never satisfy our hearts. Only God Himself can fill that blank which is made in His shape. If we will yield to this, some of us will have a new outlook on life. We will have a new zest for life, even in the dreariest surroundings . . . . The situations may not change, but we have changed. If fellowship with God is our first concern, then we can have fellowship with God in the kitchen, in sickness, in any kind of trying and difficult situation. Whatever lies across our path to be done, even the most irksome chores, are there to be done for God and for His glory. Gone will be the former striving, bondage and frustration. We shall be at peace with our God and ourselves.[1]

A Jubilant Book.

Forty years ago, Harry Emerson Fosdick had this to say about the joyousness of the New Testament:

The New Testament itself is full of troubles. It begins with a massacre of innocent children: it is centered in the crucifixion and it ends with a vision in which the souls of the martyred saints under the altar cry, "How long, O Master?" The Book was written by men whose familiar experiences were excommunications, persecutions, martyrdoms. Their faith was not like a candleflame, easily blown out by a high wind, but like a great fire fanned into a more powerful conflagration. In consequence, while the New Testament is supremely a book of hardship and tragedy, it is far and away the most exultant book in the literature of religion.[2]

The following paragraphs are quoted from *The New Harper's Bible Dictionary:*

The Bible is the most joyous book in sacred literature. The New Testament reveals Christianity as the most joyful of world religions.

Almost at the beginning of the New Testament the note of gladness was sounded. The worshipping wise men rejoiced to find again the star that had led them to Bethlehem (Matthew 2:10). Mary rejoiced that God her Saviour had looked upon her lowly estate (Luke 1:47); angels announced their "good tidings of great joy" which was to "all people" (Luke 2:10); Jesus came into the world that his joy might be established in men and made complete (John 15:11). He cured paralytics, who leaped for gladness. "For the joy that was set before him, he endured the cross" (Hebrews 12:2). When his disciples found themselves successful in furthering his Kingdom, they were filled with joy (Acts 13:52, 15:31). To Paul, the Kingdom *was* joy, as well as righteousness and peace (Romans 14:17). The fellowship of first century Christians was marked by joy as stressed in the letters of John (1 John 1:4; 2 John 12) who felt no greater happiness than hearing that his "children" were walking in the truth (3 John 4).[3]

Joy in the Gospels.

1. *Mary's Magnificat.* Early in Luke's Gospel, before he tells of the Nativity, the note of joy is clearly sounded when Mary visits her cousin Elizabeth, whose "babe leaped in her womb for joy," and who prophesied:

Blessed is she that believed: for there shall be a performance of those things which were told her from the Lord. (Luke 1:45, KJV)

It was then that Mary spoke her beautiful praise hymn, the Magnificat:

... My soul doth magnify the Lord,
And my spirit hath rejoiced in God my Saviour ....
For he that is mighty hath done to me great things; and holy is his name.
And his mercy is on them that fear him from generation to generation.
He hath shewed strength with his arm; he hath scattered the proud in the imagination of their hearts.
He hath put down the mighty from their seats, and exalted them of low degree.
He hath filled the hungry with good things; and the rich he hath sent empty away. (Luke 1:46, 47, 49-53, KJV)

2. *The Nativity.* In the fullness of time, the Old Testament prophecies were fulfilled: the baby Jesus was born in Bethlehem; and the angels announced their "good tidings of great joy" which shall be to all people. No wonder the celebration of Christmas resulted over the years in innumerable hymns trying to express the "joy unspeakable and full of glory" (1 Pet. 1:8).

3. *Songs of Joy.*

(1)
O Come, O Come, Emmanuel

O come, O come, Emmanuel,
And ransom captive Israel,
That mourns in lonely exile here
Until the Son of God appear.
  Rejoice! Rejoice! Emmanuel
  Shall come to thee, O Israel!

O come, Thou Dayspring, come and cheer
Our spirits by Thine advent here:
And drive away the shades of night,
And pierce the clouds and bring us light!
   Rejoice! Rejoice! Emmanuel
   Shall come to thee, O Israel!

O come, thou Wisdom from on high,
And order all things far and nigh;
To us the path of knowledge show,
And cause us in her ways to go.
   Rejoice! Rejoice! Emmanuel
   Shall come to thee, O Israel!

O come, Thou Key of David, come
And open wide our heavenly home:
Make safe the way that leads on high,
And close the path to misery.
   Rejoice! Rejoice! Emmanuel
   Shall come to thee, O Israel!

O come, Desire of Nations, bind
All peoples in one heart and mind:
Bid envy, strife and quarrels cease;
Fill all the world with heaven's peace.
   Rejoice! Rejoice! Emmanuel
   Shall come to thee, O Israel!
      (Latin hymn, c. 13th century
      Trans. by John M. Neale, 1851)

(2)
Joy to the World!

Joy to the world! the Lord is come:
Let earth receive her King:
Let every heart prepare Him room
And heaven and nature sing:
And heaven and nature sing.
Joy to the world! the Saviour reigns!

Let men their songs employ:
While fields and floods, rocks, hills, and plains
Repeat the sounding joy.
Repeat the sounding joy.

He rules the world with truth and grace,
And makes the nations prove
The glories of His righteousness
And wonders of His love,
And wonders of His love.
   (Isaac Watts, 1674-1748,
   From Psalm 98)

(3)
Joy to Every Waiting Heart

Hail, Thou long-expected Jesus,
 Born to set Thy people free:
From our sins and fears release us:
 Let us find our rest in Thee.

Israel's strength and consolation,
 Hope of all the saints Thou art:
Long-desired of every nation,
 Joy of every waiting heart.

Born Thy people to deliver,
 Born a child, and yet a king,
Born to reign in us forever,
 Now Thy precious kingdom bring.

By Thine own eternal Spirit
 Rule in all our hearts alone:
By Thine all-sufficient merit
 Raise us to Thy glorious throne. Amen.
   (Charles Wesley, 1707-1789)

(4)
Joy! Joy! Joy!

While by my sheep I watched by night,

Glad tidings brought an angel bright.
How great my joy! Great my joy!
  Joy, joy, joy! Joy, joy, joy!
    Praise we the Lord in heaven on high!
    Praise we the Lord in heaven on high!

There shall be born, so he did say,
In Bethlehem, a child today.
How great my joy! Great my joy!
  Joy, joy, joy! Joy, joy, joy!
    Praise we the Lord in heaven on high!
    Praise we the Lord in heaven on high!

There shall the Child lie in a stall,
This Child who shall redeem us all.
How great my joy! Great my joy!
    Praise we the Lord in heaven on high!
    Praise we the Lord in heaven on high!

This gift of God we'll cherish well,
That ever joy our hearts shall fill.
How great our joy! Great our joy!
    Praise we the Lord in heaven on high!
    Praise we the Lord in heaven on high!
  (From the German 17th century carol)

4. *Joyous Occasions in Jesus' Life.*

(1) The Trip to Jerusalem. The Gospels give us very little information about Jesus' boyhood. The one account they give us is of His trip to Jerusalem with His parents when He was a boy of twelve. And that occasion is covered in a brief twelve verses, Luke 2:40-52.

It takes only a little imagination, however, to realize something of the joy that must have been in His twelve-year-old heart, at seeing at long last the beautiful city so sacred to His people. No wonder He replied to His mother's reproachful words, "Son, why hast thou so dealt with us?" with a surprised, "How is it that ye sought me?

wist ye not that I must be about my Father's business?"

> And he went down with them, and came to Nazareth, and was subject unto them....
>
> And Jesus increased in wisdom and stature, and in favor with God and man. (Luke 2:48, 51-52, KJV)

(2) The First Miracle. It is interesting to note that Jesus' first recorded miracle—turning the water into wine (John 2:1-11)—was performed in connection with a wedding celebration, with no apparent motive other than to deepen the joy of the occasion.

Just in passing, this incident recalls a comment of Jesus when He was talking to the people about John the Baptist:

> ... Whereunto then shall I liken the men of this generation? and to what are they like?
>
> They are like unto children sitting in the marketplace, and calling to one another, and saying, We have piped unto you, and ye have not danced; we have mourned to you, and ye have not wept.
>
> For John the Baptist came neither eating bread nor drinking wine; and ye say, He hath a devil.
>
> The Son of man is come eating and drinking; and ye say, Behold, a gluttonous man and a winebibber, a friend of publicans and sinners! (Luke 7:31-34, KJV)

Surely there is indication here that Jesus found joy in the simple pleasures of life.

(3) Levi's Feast (Luke 5:27-32). In a letter written in 1884, Father Congreve has this to say about the great feast Levi, soon after his conversion, gave to Jesus:

> The feast which Levi gave to our Lord on his conversion is such a cheerful type to me of the Christian life. It is a festival of joy and gratitude for a conversion. We are

sinners forgiven: *there* is a reason for perpetual praise. A feast represents a forgiven sinner's whole course: he is welcomed home, and has brought more joy to heaven than there was before. His sorrow for sin is not a mortified, humiliated, angry disgust with himself. It is a humble, hopeful sorrow, always turning into joy . . . . So our life ought to be full of the joy of grateful love; the remembrance of sin means the remembrance of the love that called us out of our sins and forgave us the whole debt. And besides, Levi made him a great feast. It is not that we are to be cheerful for our own gratification but our life is to be full of praise and thanksgiving, singing and making melody in our hearts to the Lord, for the honour of Jesus: Levi made *Him* a feast. Our habitual joy is due to God; and our joy means not a reflection of the joy of God, but it is the very joy of God . . . . If we are sinners forgiven we ought to behave as forgiven, welcomed home, crowned with wonderful love in Christ, and so cheer and encourage all about us, who often go heavily because we reflect our gloom upon them instead of our grateful love, hope, confidence.[4]

(4) The Triumphal Entry (Luke 19:28-40), is another recorded occasion of great joy. The biblical account climaxes with these words:

And when he was come nigh . . . the whole multitude of the disciples began to rejoice and praise God with a loud voice for all the mighty works that they had seen;

Saying, Blessed be the King that cometh in the name of the Lord: peace in heaven, and glory in the highest. (Luke 19:37-38, KJV)

4

Jesus' Own Words about Joy

It is surprising to discover how much Jesus' teachings have to do with joy.

1. *The Beatitudes.*
What a strange and unexpected list of those who are "blessed"! Who but Jesus himself would ever have included in such a list "those who mourn," (Isn't that by definition a contradiction?), and "those who have been persecuted and reviled and slandered for My sake"?

If we were to write our own list of "blessed" people, how different would it be? Would it contain, "those who have great possessions," "who enjoy good health," "who are much loved and respected," "who are free from responsibilities that prevent them from doing things they want to do"?

But if we live long enough we discover that these things do not guarantee happiness. Gerald Kennedy comments:

> The unhappiest people I know are the ones with money and leisure enough to do nothing but search for happiness.[1]

"Be a Blessing."

"I will bless you," God said to Abraham, and then enumerated the ways in which he would do this for him and for his descendants. God continued, ". . . so that you will be a blessing." . . . Implicit in his blessing was the expectation of a response of obedient faith on the part of his children . . . . A true blessing doesn't stop—it spreads . . . .

Some people in trying to bring present-day relevance to the Beatitudes of Jesus . . . have suggested the substitution of the word "happy" for "blessed . . . ." Somehow the word "happy" seems inadequate. For one thing, that word has a direct relationship to the word "hap" and "happen-stance," which have the element of chance, luck, and uncertainty in them. Human happiness is often a fickle thing that fluctuates with every turn of events and every circumstance of life or fortune . . . .

Christian blessedness is a deep serene joy that exists independent of circumstances. It is a joy that abides even in the midst of sorrow, pain, grief . . . .

It is an inner peace that comes from being surrounded by the love of God and being secure in his acceptance and forgiveness. The word "blessed" has a deep spiritual significance that the word "happy" just can't convey . . . .

True blessedness depends on the right relationship between God and man, and between man and other men. True blessedness is an impossibility if we are indifferent to God and care nothing for our neighbor. But for those who would choose to "conform to the image of his Son," who would be blessed and be a blessing, the Beatitudes suggest a way of life . . . .

It is a narrow way, but it is the way of ineffable and eternal joy.[2]

Andrew Murray also has some thoughts about "Being a Blessing":

God would have . . . us made to understand that when

he blesses us, this is certainly not simply to make us happy but that we should still further communicate His blessing. God Himself is love, and therefore He blesses. Love seeketh not itself, when the love of God comes to us, it will seek others through us. The young Christian must from the beginning understand that he has received grace with the definite aim of becoming a blessing to others. Keep not for yourself what the Lord gives you for others. Offer yourself expressly and completely to the Lord to be used by Him for others; that is the way to be blessed overflowingly yourself.[3]

Every gift God gives us is to be shared. Paul expressed this truth beautifully:

Blessed be God, even the Father of our Lord Jesus Christ, the Father of mercies, and the God of all comfort;
Who comforteth us in all our tribulation, that we may be able to comfort them which are in any trouble, by the comfort wherewith we ourselves are comforted of God. (2 Cor. 1:3-4, KJV)

2. *"Be of Good Cheer."*

Jesus had miraculously fed the multitude with the five loaves and two fishes. He had then sent His disciples before Him in a ship to the other side of the lake, while He went up into a mountain to pray; and when the evening was come, He was there alone.

But the ship was now in the midst of the sea, tossed with waves: for the wind was contrary.
And in the fourth watch of the night, Jesus went unto them, walking on the sea.
And when the disciples saw him walking on the sea, they were troubled, saying, It is a spirit; and they cried out for fear.
But straightway Jesus spake unto them, saying, Be of good cheer; it is I; be not afraid. (Matt. 14:24-27, KJV)

(So Jesus speaks to each one of us today. When we are truly seeking His will for us; when we have yielded our will to His; when we are earnestly striving to follow His guidance; then He gives us such assurance of His presence that we need fear none of life's winds and storms. He is in control of every circumstance.)

3. *The Parables.*

Joy is an inescapable part of many of Jesus' most-loved parables.

In the Parable of the Talents, we remember the Lord's commendation of the faithful servant:

> ... Well done, thou good and faithful servant ... enter thou into the joy of thy Lord. (Matt. 25:21, 23, KJV)

In Luke's brief parable of the Lost Sheep, Jesus describes in unforgettable words the "joy in heaven" over one sinner that repents:

> What man of you, having an hundred sheep, if he lose one of them, doth not leave the ninety and nine in the wilderness, and go after that which is lost, until he find it?
>
> And when he hath found it, he layeth it on his shoulders, rejoicing.
>
> And when he cometh home, he calleth together his friends and neighbours, saying unto them, Rejoice with me; for I have found my sheep which was lost.
>
> I say unto you, that likewise joy shall be in heaven over one sinner that repenteth more than over ninety and nine just persons which need no repentance. (Luke 15:4-7, KJV)

The parable of the Lost Coin closes with a similar assurance:

> Likewise, I say unto you, there is joy in the presence of the angels of God over one sinner that repenteth. (Luke 15:10, KJV)

Remember too the parable of the Prodigal Son, whose return and confession of unworthiness brought from his father the following joyful declaration:

> ... Bring forth the best robe, and put it on him; and put a ring on his hand, and shoes on his feet;
>
> And bring hither the fatted calf, and kill it; and let us eat, and be merry;
>
> For this my son was dead, and is alive again; he was lost, and is found. And they began to be merry. (Luke 15:22-24, KJV)

J.B. Phillips comments on this parable as follows:

> I can imagine the Prodigal Son, making his painful way home, rehearsing again and again his speech of apology, and all the time imagining a furious father. But what really happened? "While he was yet a great way off, his father ran, and fell on his neck and kissed him."
>
> If ever a man had provoked wrath and indignation of a father, it was surely the Prodigal Son. Yet the picture of his reception by the father is given to us by Christ Himself. It is authentic.
>
> God's attitude of love cannot change.
>
> Men can hurt and punish themselves by defying his love. They can defraud and impoverish their own lives by refusing to accept his love into their hearts. They may even reach a state where his unchanging goodness, love and truth may look to them like a fearful threat (and they may call this the "wrath" of God). But even in that state they have not "provoked" him in the human sense.
>
> If we turn to God, we will find him as did the Prodigal Son.
>
> It will be: "Welcome Home!"[4]

4. *The Final Judgment.*

In Jesus' description of the final judgment, there is a lovely picture of the kind of life that wins the blessing of the Father God:

Then shall the King say unto them on his right hand, Come, ye blessed of my Father, inherit the kingdom prepared for you from the foundation of the world:

For I was an hungred, and ye gave me meat: I was thirsty and ye gave me drink: I was a stranger, and ye took me in:

Naked, and ye clothed me: I was sick, and ye visited me: I was in prison, and ye came unto me.

... Verily I say unto you, Inasmuch as ye have done it unto one of the least of these my brethren, ye have done it unto me. (Matt. 25:34-36, 40, KJV)

5. *A Promise: If* ....

If you keep my commandments, ye shall abide in my love; Even as I have kept my Father's commandments, and abide in his love.

These things I have spoken unto you, that my joy might remain in you, and that your joy might be full. (John 15:10-11, KJV)

6. *Joy through Sorrow.*

In His last recorded conversation with His disciples, before His crucifixion, Jesus warned them of His coming death, but added joyful words of comfort:

Verily, verily, I say unto you, That ye shall weep and lament, but the world shall rejoice: and ye shall be sorrowful, but your sorrow shall be turned into joy.

... Ye now therefore have sorrow: but I will see you again, and your heart shall rejoice, and your joy no man taketh from you.

In the world ye shall have tribulation: but be of good cheer; I have overcome the world. (John 16:20, 22, 33, KJV)

5

Joy in the Acts of the Apostles

1. *Pentecost.* The first two chapters in the Book of Acts record the joyous occasion of Pentecost, when the promised gift of the Holy Spirit was finally received and the new Church of Jesus had its beginning; and Peter's sermon resulted in the conversion of 3,000 people!

Peter concluded his sermon with these words:

> Therefore let all the house of Israel know assuredly, that God hath made that same Jesus, whom ye have crucified, both Lord and Christ.
>
> ... Repent, and be baptized every one of you in the name of Jesus Christ for the remission of sins, and ye shall receive the gift of the Holy Ghost.
>
> For the promise is unto you, and to your children, and to all that are afar off, even as many as the Lord our God shall call. (Acts 2:36, 38, 39, KJV)

The story goes on:

> Then they that gladly received his word were baptized: and the same day there were added unto them about three thousand souls.
>
> And they, continuing daily with one accord in the temple, and breaking bread from house to house, did eat their meat with gladness and singleness of heart,

Praising God, and having favour with all the people. (Acts 2:41, 46, 47, KJV)

2. *Peter and John.* In Acts 4 is the account of the first arrest of Peter and John for their witnessing about Jesus in the temple courtyard (4:1-3). On the following day they were called before the council, who:

... commanded them not to speak at all nor teach in the name of Jesus.

But Peter and John answered and said unto them, Whether it be right in the sight of God to hearken unto you more than unto God, judge ye.

For we cannot but speak the things which we have seen and heard. (Acts 4:18-20, KJV)

The second arrest soon took place (5:17-18):

But the angel of the Lord by night opened the prison doors, and brought them forth, and said,

Go, stand and speak in the temple to the people all the words of this life. (Acts 5:19-20, KJV)

This time their arrest and trial resulted in a beating:

And they [Peter and John] departed from the presence of the council, rejoicing that they were counted worthy to suffer shame for his name.

And daily in the temple, and in every house, they ceased not to teach and preach Jesus Christ. (Acts 5:41-42, KJV)

3. *Paul and Barnabas.* In Acts 13 is another surprising reference to joy. Paul and Barnabas, on one of their journeys, had been witnessing in Antioch and Pisidia, and had just been driven out of the city.

But they shook off the dust of their feet against them, and came unto Iconium.

And the disciples were filled with joy, and with the Holy Ghost. (Acts 13:51-52, KJV)

Joy in the Epistles of Paul.

1. *Selections from Romans.* The joy of the Christian is based upon his faith in God's love for him. Perhaps the most beautiful expression of that faith in the whole Bible is found in the following verses of this letter:

> Who shall separate us from the love of Christ? shall tribulation, or distress, or persecution, or famine, or nakedness, or peril, or sword?
> Nay, in all these things we are more than conquerors through him that loved us.
> For I am persuaded that neither death, nor life, nor angels, nor principalities, nor powers, nor things present, nor things to come,
> Nor height, nor depth, nor any other creature, shall be able to separate us from the love of God, which is in Christ Jesus our Lord. (Rom. 8:35, 37-39, KJV)

> So now, since we have been made right in God's sight by faith in his promises, we can have real peace with him because of what Jesus Christ our Lord has done for us.
> For because of our faith, he has brought us into this place of highest privilege where we now stand, and we confidently and joyfully look forward to actually becoming all that God has had in mind for us to be.
> We can rejoice, too, when we run into problems and trials for we know that they are good for us—they help us learn to be patient. And patience develops strength of character in us and helps us trust God more each time we use it . . . . (Rom. 5:1-4, TLB)

> The kingdom of God is not meat and drink; but righteousness, and peace, and joy in the Holy Ghost. (Rom. 14:17, KJV)

> May the God of hope fill you with joy and peace in your faith, that by the power of the Holy Spirit, your whole life and outlook may be radiant with hope. (Rom. 15:13, JBP)

2. *Selections from the Corinthian Letters.*

... Eye hath not seen, nor ear heard, neither have entered into the heart of man, the things which God hath prepared for them that love him. (1 Cor. 2:9, KJV)

But we all, with open face beholding as in a glass the glory of the LORD, are changed into the same image from glory to glory even as by the Spirit of the Lord. (2 Cor. 3:18, KJV)

For God, who commanded the light to shine out of darkness, hath shined in our hearts, to give the light of the knowledge of the glory of God in the face of Jesus Christ. (2 Cor. 4:6, KJV)

3. *Selection from Galatians.*

... The fruit of the Spirit is love, joy, peace, longsuffering, gentleness, goodness, faith, meekness, temperance .... (Gal. 5:22-23, KJV)

4. *Selections from Ephesians.*

For ye were sometimes darkness, but now are ye light in the LORD: walk as children of light. (Eph. 5:8, KJV)

Be filled with the Spirit;
Speaking to yourselves in psalms and hymns, and spiritual songs, singing and making melody in your heart to the Lord:
Giving thanks always for all things unto God and the Father in the name of our Lord Jesus Christ;
Submitting yourselves one to another in the fear of God. (Eph. 5:18-21, KJV)

5. *Selections from Philippians.*

Finally, my brethren, rejoice in the Lord. (Phil. 3:1, KJV)

Rejoice in the Lord alway: and again I say, Rejoice.

Finally, brethren, whatsoever things are true, whatsoever things are honest, whatsoever things are just, whatsoever things are pure, whatsoever things are lovely, whatsoever things are of good report, if there be any virtue, and if there be any praise, think on these things. (Phil. 4:4, 8, KJV)

6. *Selections from Colossians.*

For this cause we ... do not cease to pray for you ... that ye might walk worthy of the Lord unto all pleasing, being fruitful in every good work, and increasing in the knowledge of God;

Strengthened with all might according to his glorious power, unto all patience and longsuffering with joyfulness .... (Col. 1:9-11, KJV)

And now just as you trusted Christ to save you, trust him, too, for each day's problems; live in vital union with him. Let your roots grow down into him and draw up nourishment from him. See that you go on growing in the Lord, and become strong and vigorous in the truth you were taught. Let your lives overflow with joy and thanksgiving for all he has done. (Col. 2:6-7, TLB)

If ye then be risen with Christ, seek those things which are above, where Christ sitteth on the right hand of God.

Set your affection on things above, not on things on the earth.

For ye are dead, and your life is hid with Christ in God.

When Christ, who is our life, shall appear, then shall ye also appear with him in glory. (Col. 3:1-4, KJV)

Let Christ's teaching live in your hearts, making you rich in the true wisdom. Teach and help one another along the right road with your psalms and hymns and Christian songs, singing God's praises with joyful hearts. And whatever work you may have to do, do everything in the name of the Lord Jesus, thanking God the Father through him. (Col. 3:16-17, JBP)

7. *Selections from First Thessalonians.*

Ye are all the children of light, and the children of day: we are not of the night, nor of darkness. (1 Thess. 5:5, KJV)

Rejoice evermore.
In every thing give thanks: for this is the will of God in Christ Jesus concerning you. (1 Thess. 5:16, 18, KJV)

8. *Selection from Timothy.*

... Trust ... in the living God, who giveth us richly all things to enjoy. (1 Tim. 6:17, KJV)

Joy in the General Epistles.

1. *Selections from Hebrews.*

For unto which of the angels said he at any time, Thou art my Son, this day have I begotten thee? ...

Thou hast loved righteousness, and hated iniquity; therefore God, even thy God, hath anointed thee with the oil of gladness above thy fellows .... (Heb. 1:5, 9, KJV)

Wherefore seeing we also are compassed about with so great a cloud of witnesses, let us lay aside every weight, and the sin which doth so easily beset us, and let us run with patience the race that is set before us.

Looking unto Jesus the author and finisher of our faith; who for the joy that was set before him endured the cross, despising the shame, and is set down at the right hand of the throne of God. (Heb. 12:1-2, KJV)

2. *Selection from James.*

My brethren, count it all joy when you fall into divers temptations;
Knowing this, that the trying of your faith worketh patience.
But let patience have her perfect work, that ye may be perfect and entire, wanting nothing. (James 1:2-4, KJV)

3. *Selections from First Peter.*

Blessed be the God and Father of our Lord Jesus Christ, which according to his abundant mercy hath begotten us again unto a lively hope by the resurrection of Jesus Christ from the dead,

To an inheritance incorruptible, and undefiled, and that fadeth not away, reserved in heaven for you,

Who are kept by the power of God through faith unto salvation ready to be revealed in the last time.

Wherein ye greatly rejoice, though now for a season, if need be, ye are in heaviness through manifold temptations:

That the trial of your faith, being much more precious than of gold that perisheth, though it be tried with fire, might be found unto praise and honour and glory at the appearing of Jesus Christ:

Whom having not seen, ye love; in whom, though now ye see him not, yet believing, ye rejoice with joy unspeakable and full of glory . . . . (1 Pet. 1:3-8, KJV)

. . . Ye are a chosen generation, a royal priesthood, an holy nation, a peculiar people; that ye should shew forth the praises of him who hath called you out of darkness into his marvellous light:

Which in time past were not a people, but are now the people of God: which had not obtained mercy, but now have obtained mercy. (1 Pet. 2:9-10, KJV)

Beloved, think it not strange concerning the fiery trial which is to try you, as though some strange thing happened unto you:

But rejoice, inasmuch as ye are partakers of Christ's sufferings; that, when his glory shall be revealed, ye may be glad also with exceeding joy. (1 Pet. 4:12, KJV)

4. *Selection from First John.*

That which was from the beginning, which we have heard, which we have seen with our eyes, which we have looked upon, and our hands have handled, of the Word of life; . . .

That which we have seen and heard declare we unto you, that ye also may have fellowship with us: and truly our fellowship is with the Father, and with his Son Jesus Christ.

And these things write we unto you, that your joy may be full.

This then is the message which we have heard of him and declare unto you, that God is light, and in him is no darkness at all. (1 John 1:1, 3, 5, KJV)

5. *Selection from Jude.*

Now unto him that is able to keep you from falling, and to present you faultless before the presence of his glory with exceeding joy,

To the only wise God our Saviour, be glory and majesty, dominion and power, both now and ever. Amen. (Jude 24-25, KJV)

Joy in Revelation.

And I heard as it were the voice of a great multitude, and as the voice of many waters, and as the voice of mighty thunderings, saying, Alleluia: for the Lord God omnipotent reigneth.

Let us be glad and rejoice, and give honour to him . . . . (Rev. 19:6-7a, KJV)

And I saw a new heaven and a new earth: for the first heaven and the first earth were passed away; and there was no more sea.

And I heard a great voice out of heaven saying, Behold, the tabernacle of God is with men, and he will dwell with them, and they shall be his people, and God himself shall be with them, and be their God.

And God shall wipe away all tears from their eyes; and there shall be no more death, neither sorrow, nor crying, neither shall there be any more pain: for the former things are passed away. . . . Behold, I make all things new. (Rev. 21:1, 3-5, KJV)

Summary: Light and Darkness.
"In the Scriptures light and gladness are frequently connected with each other. It is so in nature. The joyful light of the morning awakens the birds to their song and gladdens the watchers who in the darkness have longed for the day. It is the light of God's countenance that gives the Christian his gladness. In fellowship with his Lord he can, and always will, be happy. The love of the Father shines like the sun upon His children. When darkness comes over the soul, it is always through one of two things—through sin or through unbelief. Sin is darkness and makes dark; and unbelief also makes dark, for it turns us from Him who alone is the light . . . .

"Christians who would walk according to the will of the Lord, hear what His Word says: 'Finally, my brethren, rejoice in the Lord . . . Rejoice in the Lord alway: again, I will say, Rejoice.' (Phil. 3:1, 4, RSV) In the Lord Jesus there is joy unspeakable and full of glory. Believing in Him, rejoice in this. Live the life of faith, that life is salvation and glorious joy. A heart that gives itself undividedly to follow Jesus, that lives by faith in Him and His love, shall have light and gladness . . . . Do not seek gladness . . . But seek Jesus, follow Jesus, believe in Jesus, and gladness shall be added to you. 'Not seeing, but believing, rejoice with joy unspeakable and full of glory.'

"Lord Jesus, Thou art the light of the world, the effulgence of the unapproachable light, in whom we see the light of God. From thy countenance radiates upon us the illumination of the knowledge of the love and glory of

God. And Thou art ours, our light and our salvation. O teach us to believe more firmly that with Thee we can never walk in the darkness. Let gladness in Thee be the proof that Thou art all to us and our strength to do all that Thou wouldst have us do. Amen."[1] (Andrew Murray. In *The New Life*)

Part II

Living With Joy:
the Christian's Responsibility

6

Jesus' Directives: The "Good and Satisfying Things"

The dictionary defines *joy* as the "emotion produced by something good and satisfying." We cannot read far in the gospels without discovering in Jesus' teachings just what "the good and satisfying things" are—those conditions which, when fulfilled, will inevitably flood our hearts with His joy.

The Two Commandments.
Early in the history of the Jews, God gave them, through Moses, the Ten Commandments as a basis for their law (see Exodus 20:1-17). It is interesting to note that when Jesus was asked which was the most important commandment He mentioned *two*—neither one of which appears, in the form He stated it, in the "Ten." (See Deuteronomy 6:5, and Leviticus 19:18.)

J.B. Phillips translates the story like this:

> Then one of the scribes approached him . . . and . . . he put this question to him.
> "What are we to consider the greatest commandment of all?"

"The first and most important one is this," Jesus replied—" *'Hear, O Israel: The Lord our God, the Lord is one: and thou shalt love the Lord thy God with all thy heart, and with all thy soul, and with all thy mind, and with all thy strength.'* The second is this, *'Thou shalt love thy neighbor as thyself.'* No other commandment is greater than these."

"I am well answered," replied the scribe. "You are absolutely right when you say that there is one God and no other God exists but him; and to love him with the whole of our hearts, the whole of our intelligence and the whole of our energy, and to love our neighbors as ourselves is infinitely more important than all these burnt offerings and sacrifices."

Then Jesus, noting the thoughtfulness of his reply said to him, "You are not far from the kingdom of God!" (Mark 12:28-34, JBP)

In his book *For This Day* J.B. Phillips has this comment under the heading of "Self-love":

> The second great commandment is that a man should "love his neighbor as himself."
>
> These words, I am sure, contain no accidental lapse of speech. We do naturally love ourselves, and no spiritual contortions or inverted pride can ever alter the fact. Surely what Jesus is urging is that that love, that understanding, that "making allowance," which we normally use for ourselves, should be extended and used to embrace others . . . .
>
> The business of hating oneself, though it appears virtuous, is in reality one of Satan's most plausible devices.
>
> It keeps a man preoccupied with himself and his sins.

Specific Directives.

Later on in His teaching, Jesus separated these two

laws into a number of specific directives. These are concerned with attitudes and actions which, if we persistently live by them, will prove to be the "good and satisfying things" which inevitably fill our hearts with Christian joy, that joy which is "unspeakable and full of glory" (1 Pet. 1:8).

1. "Seek First the Kingdom."

... Take no thought, saying, what shall we eat? or, What shall we drink? or, Wherewithal shall we be clothed?

... for your Heavenly Father knoweth that ye have need of all these things.

But seek ye first the kingdom of God, and his righteousness; and all these things shall be added unto you.

Take therefore no thought for the morrow: for the morrow shall take thought for the things of itself. Sufficient unto the day is the evil thereof. (Matt. 6:31-34, KJV)

This first directive implies a number of others. How do we "seek the kingdom of God"? Obviously by a study of God's Word; by turning to God in prayer and praise; by associating ourselves intimately with some part of His Body, the Church, and becoming actively involved in some ministry of service.

To aid you in this search, there is provided a section of choice prayers for you to use in enriching your private devotions, some biblical, some from the "saints," some prayer hymns. (See Part IV: "OUR FATHER: PRAYERS OF FAITH AND JOY.")

2. The Golden Rule.

... All things whatsoever ye would that men should do to you, do ye even so to them .... (Matt. 7:12, KJV)

This directive implies an ability to put yourself in the place of another. An old Indian prayer has a similar emphasis: "Great Spirit, grant that I may not criticize my neighbor, until I have walked a mile in his moccasins."

3. *"Judge Not."*

Judge not, that ye be not judged. For with what judgment ye judge, ye shall be judged . . . . (Matt. 7:1-2, KJV)

This is one of the hardest of the directives to live by. Too many of us have the self-righteousness of the Pharisee who "prayed":

"Thank God, I am not a sinner like everyone else, especially like that tax collector over there! For I never cheat, I don't commit adultery, I go without food twice a week, and I give to God a tenth of everything I earn." (Luke 18:11-12, TLB)

4. *"Forgive."*

Then came Peter to him, and said, Lord, how oft shall my brother sin against me, and I forgive him? till seven times?
Jesus saith unto him, I say not unto thee, Until seven times: but, Until seventy times seven. (Matt. 18:21-22, KJV)

Perhaps the hardest part of true forgiveness is *forgetfulness*, and no forgiveness is complete without that. *God's* forgiveness always includes forgetfulness.

For I will be merciful to their unrighteousness, and their sins and their iniquities will I remember no more. (Heb. 8:12, KJV)

5. *"Go the Second Mile."*

And whosoever shall compel thee to go a mile, go with him twain. (Matt. 5:41, KJV)

In Jesus' day, any Roman soldier could legally command any man in a conquered country to carry his pack for one mile. Under those circumstances, *going the second mile* was almost unthinkable!

But in our life today, going the second mile means *doing more than we are expected to do*, fulfilling all our responsibilities and going beyond; seeing what needs to be done, and doing it *without being asked*.

6. *"Love Your Enemy."*

Ye have heard that it hath been said, Thou shalt love thy neighbour, and hate thine enemy.

But I say unto you, Love your enemies, bless them that curse you, do good to them that hate you, and pray for them which despitefully use you, and persecute you,

That ye may be the children of your Father which is in heaven: for he maketh his sun to rise on the evil and on the good, and sendeth rain on the just and on the unjust. (Matt. 5:43-45, KJV)

No other of Jesus' directives is ignored as this one is. From the world's standpoint this is utter idiocy, an impossible requirement. And yet God's Word is clear and distinct, as is Jesus' example on the cross.

7

Jesus' Directives (Concluded)

7. *"Be the Servant of All."*
Jesus' disciples had much to learn as followers of their Master. Perhaps no incident reveals this more clearly than their concern as to which of them would be greatest in His Kingdom. When Jesus discovered that they were discussing this, He called them all to Him and said:

> You know that the so-called rulers in the heathen world lord it over them, and their great men have absolute power. But it must not be so among you. No, whoever among you wants to be great must become the servant of you all, and if he wants to be first among you he must be the slave of all men! For the Son of Man himself has not come to be served, but to serve. (Mark 10:44, JBP)

"The servant of all" is not an appointment many of us are willing to accept! Relevant to this is an incident described by Gerald Kennedy:

> In one of our church hospitals in a very exclusive community, we have more women who have volunteered their services than we can possibly use. There is nothing to gain from their service so far as personal advantage is concerned and there certainly is no prestige to be gained. But hundreds of well-to-do women both young and old

stand ready to give time and energy to the sick just because they are needed. When a young woman was doing a particularly dirty job, a society lady said, "I wouldn't do that for a thousand dollars," and the young woman glancing up replied, "Neither would I."[1]

Why then *did* she do it? Obviously she had been caught by a vision of the beauty and importance of Christian service. She was *living* (being a doer of) the word of Christ. Thousands of saints through the ages have found a similar joyous fulfillment in obedience to Jesus' call to humble servitude.

"The Romance of Stewardship."
The total dedication of ourselves and our abilities to Jesus for use in His ministry of service, including the dedication of our material possessions. Christian stewardship of our worldly possessions provides us with an opportunity of sharing in the worldwide ministry of Jesus, as Harry Emerson Fosdick reminded us over fifty years ago:

> Once in an isolated settlement of the old world of slow communication, a man could hear of cruel need in the antipodes and go home with nothing but sympathy to offer. Let no man in this modern world express sympathy with any need anywhere on earth unless he *means* it! The acid test can straightway be applied. For we can *do something*, no matter where the need may be. The agencies of human helpfulness work over all the earth. The avenues are open down which our pennies, our dollars, or our millions can walk together in an accumulating multitude to the succor of all mankind. Each of us can take some of his own merit and sinew reduced in wages to the form of money, and through money which is a naturalized citizen of all lands, and which speaks all languages, can be at work wherever the sun shines. It is a

privilege which no one knew before our modern world. It is one of the miracles of science mastered by the spirit of service, that a man busy at his daily tasks at home can yet be preaching the Gospel in Alaska, healing the sick in Korea, teaching in the schools of Persia, feeding the hungry in India, and building a new civilization at the headwaters of the Nile. Only a man with generous, systematic stewardship in taking advantage of the new opportunities is fully abreast of his times.[2]

God's Instrument.

Perhaps no more satisfying description of what it means to be the "servant of all" has ever been written than the inspired prayer of St. Francis of Assisi:

Lord, make me an instrument of Thy peace.
 Where there is hatred, let me sow love;
 where there is injury, pardon;
 where there is doubt, faith;
 where there is despair, hope;
 where there is sadness, joy;
 where there is darkness, light.
O Divine Master, grant that I may not so much seek
 to be consoled, as to console;
 not so much to be understood as to understand;
 not so much to be loved, as to love;
 For it is in giving that we receive;
 it is in pardoning that we are pardoned;
 it is in dying that we are born again to eternal life.

Alan Paton writes:

No Christian should ever think or say that he is not fit to be God's instrument—that in fact is what it means to be a Christian. We may be humble about many things, but we must never decline to be used . . . .

The gospel is full of reassurances to us, some of them startling: You are salt to the world! You are light! Even the hairs of your head have all been counted! These words were exciting to those who heard them .... They were given a new sense of their value as persons .... One can hardly describe the joy of the first disciples, who were given by Jesus such a sense of their significance in the world. This same sense of significance has been given again and again to other people by disciples of Jesus.

In the same book the author writes:

"Lord, I believe, help thou mine unbelief" (Mark 9:14-24, KJV).

That indeed is the cry of many of us for our faith is many times put to the test, by the failure of our ideals to triumph, by the long illness of some beloved person, by world disasters, by wars and rumours of wars. "Why does God allow it?" is a question one often hears. "Is God really a loving God when he permits such things to happen? Can God really be all-powerful? For if he is all-powerful, then he cannot be loving."

As far as we know, Francis of Assisi never asked himself these questions. If there was sorrow, he asked to be allowed to bring joy. If there was darkness, he asked to be allowed to bring light. If there was grief, he asked to be allowed to bring comfort. This concept of discipleship was sublime.[3]

In his first meditation on St. Francis' prayer (in the same book) Alan Paton pays tribute to St. Francis:

I wish to place on record that I am in unrepayable debt to Francis of Assisi, for when I pray his prayer, or even remember it, my melancholy is dispelled, my self-pity comes to an end, my faith is restored, because of this majestic conception of what the work of a disciple should be ....

And I say to myself, this is the only way in which a Christian can encounter hatred, injury, despair, and sadness, and that is by throwing off his helplessness and allowing himself to be made the bearer of love, the pardoner, the bringer of hope, the comforter of those who grieve.[4]

Jesus' Own Description of His Ministry.

In reading the above, I was reminded of Jesus' own description of His ministry when John the Baptist sent two of his disciples to ask Jesus this question:

> ... Art thou he that should come? or look we for another? ...
>
> Then Jesus answering said unto them, Go your way, and tell John what things ye have seen and heard; how that the blind see, the lame walk, the lepers are cleansed, the deaf hear, the dead are raised, to the poor the Gospel is preached. (Luke 7:19, 22, KJV)

The Church's Ministry Today.

This description of Jesus' ministry describes the task of the Church today. It is our ministry as part of the "Body of Christ." "Become the servant of all." When the Church takes literally this command of Jesus, God's Kingdom will have come on earth.

8. *"Take Up Your Cross and Follow Me."*

The eighth and last selected directive of Jesus, completing the list of conditions which produce His joy, is stated in each of the three synoptic gospels.

> Then said Jesus unto his disciples, If any man will come after me, let him deny himself, and take up his cross, and follow me. (Matt. 16:24, KJV)

This saying is also found in Mark 8:14 and in Luke 9:23. (Luke adds "daily" after the word "cross.") It also occurs in Mark's account of Jesus' conversation with the rich young ruler:

Then Jesus beholding him loved him, and said unto him, one thing thou lackest: go thy way, sell whatsoever thou hast, and give to the poor, and thou shalt have treasure in heaven: and come, take up thy cross, and follow me. (Mark 10:21, KJV)

Again, in Matthew 10:38, this directive is stated, this time negatively:

... he that taketh not his cross, and followeth after me, is not worthy of me.

The Living Bible paraphrases it:

If you refuse to take up your cross and follow me, you are not worthy of being mine.

What does it mean to take up your cross? "Cross" is sometimes applied to any affliction, or trial, or suffering, which comes to us in life, but there is an implication in these verses that we sometimes miss. *"Take up your cross"* implies a definite *choice*. We cannot choose whether or not we will "take up" the usual calamities that befall us, the handicaps suffered in "accidents," the epidemic diseases, the loss of dear ones, the business failures, or any of the long list of trials and tribulations. We have no choice as to these things, except in what our response to them may be.

But "the cross" is different. Jesus could have escaped the cross. He chose not to. He deliberately "took it up." He accepted it because of His unswerving commitment to follow His Father's will for His life: "Not my will but thine be done."

So the challenge to us in this directive is clear. God provides certain opportunities in every life, certain challenges to "be a blessing," to be used by Him for His great purposes. He provides the challenges, but the choice is left to us. He never forces us. He leads us.

"To take up the cross" means such a firm and unyielding devotion to Jesus our Lord, that no matter where He leads through whatever trials or sufferings, we follow Him willingly, joyfully, sacrificially.

Thomas Kelly once wrote:

> I dare not urge you to your cross. But He, more powerfully, speaks within you and me ... and disquiets us with the world's needs. By inner persuasions He draws us to a few very definite tasks, our tasks, God's burdened heart particularizing His burdens in us. And He gives us the royal blindness of faith, and the seeing eye of the sensitized soul, and the grace of unflinching obedience. Then we see ... that this my task matters for me and for my fellow men and for Eternity.[5]

"I'll Go with Him."
I can hear my Saviour calling,
I can hear my Saviour calling,
I can hear my Saviour calling,
"Take thy cross and follow me."

Where He leads me I will follow,
Where He leads me I will follow,
Where He leads me I will follow,
I'll go with Him, with Him, all the way.[6]

In Conclusion.
Malcolm Muggeridge has some thoughts about the value of trials and afflictions:

1

Contrary to what might be expected, I look back on experiences that at the time seemed especially desolating and painful with particular satisfaction. Indeed I can say with complete truthfulness that everything that has truly enhanced and enlightened my existence, has been through affliction and not through happiness, either pursued or attained. In other words, if it ever were to be possible to eliminate affliction from our earthly existence by means of some drug, or other medical mumbo jumbo ... the result would not be to make life delectable, but to make it too banal and trivial to be endurable. This, of course, is what the Cross signifies. It is the Cross, more than anything else, that has called me inexorably to Christ. ...

2

The promises Jesus made are still valid, and will continue so to be. Particularly true is His promise that He would not disappear from the world after His death, but continue to be accessible to those who sought Him. "Lo, I am with you always," He said to the disciples, "even unto the end of the world." So it follows that in the afflictions of this world no one needs ever lack a comforter in the hardships ... no one needs ever lack a helper in the stumblings and losing of one's way, which are inevitable in the world, no one needs ever lack an arm to lean on, a guide to show the way.

3

As one more poor pilgrim who has found his way belatedly to Galilee, a true child of his time with a skeptical mind and sensual disposition, let me then add my testimony to that of millions upon millions of others during the last twenty centuries. So, I say that the words Jesus spoke and the revelation He proclaimed were true when he spoke them, are true now,. and will be true forever. Moreover, they provide for all who care to heed them a release from the fantasy of power, which is the world, transporting them into the reality of love, which is the kingdom not of this world that Jesus proclaimed. "Heaven and earth shall pass away," Jesus said, "but my words shall not pass away." We have them still our most precious heritage. Here and now, those who care to live by and in them, while still living in our earthly city, can prepare themselves for the citizenship of the city of God which lies before them.

And they may know here and now in their present experience "the joy unspeakable and full of glory."[7]

Summary.

We have concluded our consideration of eight "good and satisfying things," directives Jesus gave, which, if followed, will inevitably produce in us His joy:

The Two Commandments: Love God; Love your neighbour.

Eight Specific Directives:
1. Seek first the Kingdom (Matt. 6:31-34).
2. The Golden Rule (Matt. 7:12).
3. Judge not (Matt. 7:1-2).
4. Forgive (Matt. 18:21-22).
5. Go the second mile (Matt. 5:41).
6. Love your enemy (Matt. 5:43-45).
7. Be the servant of all (Mark 10:44).
8. Take up your cross and follow Me (Matt. 16:24).

Malcolm Smith comments:

> Jesus bequeathed His joy to the disciples. "These things have I spoken to you that my joy may be in you, and that your joy may be full" (John 15:11). Later that same night he reassured them, "Therefore you, too, now have sorrow, but I will see you again, and your heart will rejoice, and no one takes your joy away from you" (John 16:22). This was a joy not known in the darkness, a new kind of joy centered not in self but in God and His glory. This joy could never become *unjoy*, it was more real than all the sorrows that could assault it. Its object, and therefore its source, was the unchanging God.[8]

A Suggested Self-Discipline.

A true Christian by definition is a follower of Jesus

Christ, one who has been gripped by the reality of the Father God as Jesus revealed Him; one who is achieving the skill of living, as Jesus did, continually in awareness of His holy companionship; one who has accepted Jesus as his personal Savior and Master; one who has been filled with His Holy Spirit; and who has learned to trust in God's love and in all His promises, including His promise of joy.

Jesus said:

> Blessed [joyous] . . . are those who hear the word of God and keep it. (Luke 11:28, RSV)

A worthwhile self-discipline would be to read over every morning the summary of the selected directives of Jesus until they are firmly embedded in your heart and mind; and to check over them each evening to see which ones you have consciously chosen to live by and which ones you have failed to "observe" during the day.

You could not possibly follow this procedure conscientiously, for even a few days, without feeling in your heart an upsurge of the joy of the Lord.

O Love That Wilt Not Let Me Go

O Love that wilt not let me go,
   I rest my weary soul in Thee.
I give Thee back the life I owe
That in Thine ocean depths its flow
   May richer, fuller be.

O Light that followest all my way,
   I yield my flickering torch to Thee.
My heart restores its borrowed ray,
That in Thy sunshine's blaze its ray
   May brighter, fairer be.

O Joy, that seekest me through pain,
   I cannot close my heart to Thee,

I trace the rainbow through the rain,
And feel the promise is not vain,
   That morn shall tearless be.
O Cross that liftest up my head,
   I dare not ask to fly from thee:
I lay in dust life's glory dead,
And from the ground there blossoms red
   Life that shall endless be.[9]

8

Living With Joy: Our Responsibility as Christians

We have considered the "good and satisfying things" that Jesus teaches that will inevitably result in filling our hearts with His "joy unspeakable and full of glory." And we have been thinking of this joy as a blessed gift to us as the consummation of a process of living in accordance with Jesus' teachings.

Joy: An Equipment for Action.
This is all true but a further insight is needed. This joy is not a gift given to us for our selfish enjoyment. It is far more than that. It is *an equipment for action.*

Christian joy has been given to us as we have yielded our lives to Jesus; as we have committed ourselves to become part of His Body to share in His task of winning the world to himself. When we recognize this truth we face the challenging fact that *living with joy* is the Christian's responsibility, and his most effective tool in fulfilling his life's purpose.

Leslie Newbegin comments:

The Bible presents to us the picture of a people committed to God and to His Kingdom. In the Old Testament Israel is called to be such a people, not just for their own blessing, but for the blessing of the nations. They are to be a kingdom of priests for God, to mediate both his rule and his forgiveness to all the nations. They are to be witnesses to the nations who do not know God. They are to be a light to the nations and bearers of salvation to the ends of the earth.[1]

God has revealed his whole mind and purpose in Christ Jesus, supremely in his death and resurrection. In him God's whole heart and will is committed to the healing of the world. And Jesus has invited us to become part of that healing through being part of that dying and rising.... Through him and with him we offer up ourselves and our possessions and our prayers on behalf of all men, joining our prayers to his that God's kingdom may come. And then we go out to share completely and fully in the life of the world, not as a separate community seeking our own ends, different from the ends of the world, but simply as those who know what the true end of man is, and who follow Jesus serving, suffering, and witnessing, so that God's Kingdom may come and God's will may be done in all men and for all men.[2]

The Christian whose heart is flooded with "the joy of the Lord" is superbly equipped to witness convincingly to every life he touches, the truth that:

> God so loved the world, that he gave his only begotten Son, that whosoever believeth in him should not perish, but have everlasting life. (John 3:16, KJV)

Another Paradox.

Two statements which have been made seem at first glance contradictory. We have said that no one can find joy by seeking it directly because it is a by-product. And yet we are stating that living with joy is our responsibility as Christians.

If it is impossible for us to attain joy by seeking it, how can it be our responsibility to "live with joy"? Surely, we cannot be held responsible for living with joy, if no amount of striving and effort will enable us to find joy?

But the seeming contradiction is easily resolved. Although we cannot attain joy by seeking it directly, we *can* become joyous people by faithfully fulfilling those conditions which, when fulfilled, inevitably flood our hearts with the joy of the Lord.

It *is* possible so to discipline ourselves that the thoughts of our minds, the meditations of our hearts, the words we speak, the attitudes we hold, the deeds we do, are increasingly the result of our continuous awareness of "the holy companionship of God." And the nearer we approach that ideal for our lives, the more surely will the "joy unspeakable and full of glory" become our daily experience, no matter what the circumstances of our lives may be.

Hannah Whitall Smith, in a book written about a hundred years ago, says:

> A cross Christian, or an anxious Christian, a discouraged gloomy Christian, a doubting Christian, a selfish Christian, a cruel, hard-hearted Christian, a self-indulgent Christian, a Christian with a sharp tongue or bitter spirit, all these may be very earnest in their work, and may have honorable places in the Church, but they are *not* Christlike Christians.[3]

A Personal Testimony.
Jesus' joy becomes our own only when our relationship to Jesus himself is right. M. Basilea Schlink gives a moving testimony of her personal relationship with Jesus:

Since I have learned to love Jesus, my life has become unspeakably rich and happy. In Him is fullness of contentment.... No more could suffering and the cross come upon me as an oppressive power. For now I had learned to go the way of the cross. His love for me and mine for Him had transformed the cross.

In the measure that my love to Jesus grew, people and the things of this world became unimportant; they no longer held me in bondage.... More and more I became independent of anything the world could give or take away. Jesus became everything to me.

The portals of heaven opened, wider and wider. The glory of heaven shone forth.... Jesus lives in heaven. If you seek Him, you will find Him there, at the right hand of God. And finding Him, you will find all heaven![4]

A Prayer Hymn.

Frances R. Havergal's lovely prayer hymn has defined for untold numbers of people, the meaning of this kind of dedication to Jesus:

Take my life and let it be
Consecrated, Lord, to Thee;
Take my hands and let them move
At the impulse of Thy love.

Take my feet, and let them be
Swift and beautiful for Thee;
Take my voice, and let me sing
Always, only, for my King.

Take my silver and my gold,
Not a mite would I withhold;
Take my moments and my days,
Let them flow in ceaseless praise.

Take my will and make it Thine,
It shall be no longer mine;
Take my heart, it is Thine own,
It shall be Thy royal throne.[5]

Our "Great Task of Happiness"

Robert Louis Stevenson sensed the truth that joyous living is the responsibility of the Christian, as is evidenced by the following prayer poem:

If I have faltered more or less
In my great task of happiness,
If I have moved among my race
And shown no glorious morning face,
Lord, Thy most pointed pleasure take
And stab my spirit broad awake.[6]

What *is* a "pointed pleasure"? Surely the poet must have had in mind some of those painful but enlightening experiences which, from a worldly point of view, seem to be utterly tragic, but which viewed from a later time are seen to have resulted in totally unexpected values:

A business failure, which forces a man to reconsider the whole meaning of life, and results in a deep religious experience;

A term in prison which amazingly transforms an evildoer into a dedicated Christian;

The death of a loved one, which results in a whole, new orientation of life for the bereaved family through an unexpected realization that "underneath are the everlasting arms":

A serious illness, or a bad accident, which puts up a roadblock to a present life of sin, and forces a new appraisal of life's meaning;

A wrecked love affair which shatters a woman's self-esteem, but leads to the discovery of God's sufficiency for every need;

A crippling handicap that, when accepted, leads to a life of unexpected blessedness for all involved.

"Stabbing" by whatever instrument, even by a "pointed pleasure," is never without pain.

What God Hath Promised.

> God hath not promised
> Skies always blue,
> Flower-strewn pathways
> All our lives through;
> God hath not promised
> Sun without rain,
> Joy without sorrow,
> Peace without pain.
>
> But God hath promised
> Strength for the day
> Rest for the labor
> Light for the way
> Grace for the trials,
> Help from above,
> Unfailing sympathy,
> Undying love.
>   —Annie Johnson Flint

And we might add, God has also promised us "His joy" amid all the difficult and even tragic circumstances of our lives. *Christian* joy, the "joy of the Lord," is indestructible. It is a mixture of joy and sorrow, of pain and peace. It is a spiritual rainbow, impossible without both "rain" and "sun."

9

Living With Joy: Our Responsibility as Christians (Continued)

The Magnetism of the Holy Spirit in a Joyous Christian.
We have said that the "joy of the Lord" is given us to equip us for action. As a means of drawing people to Christ, no quality of living is as powerfully attractive as the outward evidence of joy and love which is the result of the indwelling Holy Spirit. The Holy Spirit is a powerful spiritual magnet.

A Twelve-Year-Old's Perception.
The power of a Spirit-filled Christian was brought strikingly to my attention some years ago by a conversation I overheard in a family situation. The family had recently been drawn into a church fellowship whose pastor was a truly radiant Christian. The father and mother were telling another couple about their experience. Their son was listening, and at one point he broke into the conversation to announce: "You know, if there's something bothering you when you go to church, just looking at pastor makes you feel better!" What an accolade!

A Memory.
A somewhat similar experience of my own comes often to my mind, although the seemingly unimportant incident happened over three-quarters of a century ago.

I was probably about six years old. I was riding my tricycle up and down on the sidewalk in front of our home one day when our minister[1] was walking by, and stopped to talk with me. He was very tall and leaned down to take my hand in his. I have no recollection of a single word he said but I vividly recall the radiance of his face, and the feeling of his encompassing love and joy as he spoke to me.

A Two-Year-Old's Response.
This brief memory flashed across my mind not long ago, when I was on a trip back to New Jersey, and attended a church with my grandson and his wife. It is a non-denominational fellowship, most of the members are Spirit-filled, and the minister is another radiant Christian.

We reached the church in good time, and settled ourselves in a front pew. Only a few early-comers had arrived. The minister knelt in prayer at the front of the church, folded his arms on the platform, and bowed his head on his folded arms. A small boy, about two years old, was wandering aimlessly around. He climbed the steps at one side of the platform and looked the situation over. Suddenly he spied the minister, still kneeling in prayer. The tot toddled over and stood a few feet away, looking at the minister curiously. Then suddenly he dropped to his knees and crawled slowly across the platform, until his head gently bumped into the bowed head of the minister! The startled man lifted his head to find himself eye to eye with the toddler. And I have no words adequately to describe the glow on his countenance as he took the child's face into his hands, held it a moment, his eyes shining into the tot's eyes with a wealth of love and acceptance. Then he folded his arms again, bowed his head and continued his prayer. And the toddler, completely satisfied, wandered off.

Sermons We See.

We have said that the joy of the Lord has been given us to "equip us for action." As a means of drawing people to Jesus Christ, one radiant Christian, filled with the joy of the Lord, living out his joyous faith in his daily life, is more effective than many who are trying to witness by words alone. The true Christian radiates such joy that people are irresistibly drawn to him, and often *ask the reason* for his joyousness. *Then* his verbal witness falls on good soil and bears fruit. Edgar Guest presents this idea persuasively in his poem below:

> I'd rather see a sermon than hear one any day.
> I'd rather one should walk with me than merely tell the way.
> The eye's a better pupil, and more willing than the ear,
> Fine counsel is confusing, but example's always clear;
> And the best of all the preachers are the ones
>   who live their creeds,
> For to see good put in action is what everybody needs.
> I soon can learn to do it if you'll let me see it done:
> I can watch your hands in action, but your tongue
>   too fast may run:
> And the lecture you deliver may be very wise and true,
> But I'd rather get my lessons by observing what you do:
> For I might misunderstand you, and the high advice you
>   give
> But there's no misunderstanding how you act and how
>   you live.

When I see a deed of kindness, I am eager to be kind.
When a weaker brother stumbles and a strong man stays
   behind
Just to see if he can help him, then the wish grows strong
   in me
To become as big and thoughtful as I know that friend to be.
And all travelers can witness that the best of guides today
Is not the one who tells them, but the one who shows the
   way.

One good man teaches many, men believe what they
   behold:
One deed of kindness noticed is worth forty that are told.
Who stands with men of honor learns to hold his honor dear,
For right living speaks a language which to everyone is
   clear.
Though an able speaker charms me with his eloquence,
   I say
I'd rather see a sermon than to hear one, any day.[2]

Jesus' Sermons Without Words.
That Jesus' whole life was a series of sermons without words is obvious to anyone who reads the gospels. An outstanding illustration of this is the incident recorded in John 13:

> Jesus knowing that the Father had given all things into his hands, and that he was come from God, and went to God;
> He riseth from supper, and laid aside his garments; and took a towel, and girded himself.
> After that he poureth water into a bason, and began to wash the disciples' feet, and to wipe them with the towel wherewith he was girded.

(Does it seem likely that any disciple present could have failed to understand that sermon even without Jesus' concluding words of explanation?)

> So after he had washed their feet, and had taken his garments, and was set down again, he said unto them, Know ye what I have done to you?
>
> Ye call me Master and Lord: and ye say well; for so I am.
>
> If I then, your Lord and Master, have washed your feet; ye also ought to wash one another's feet.
>
> For I have given you an example, that ye should do as I have done to you. (John 13:3-5, 12-15, KJV)

In Conclusion: Our Threefold Heritage.

Jesus' Gift of Joy.

We have said that our experience of "the joy of the Lord" is not just for our own selfish pleasure, but that it is an "equipment for action." The responsibility to live with joy is ours because we have received from Jesus a threefold inheritance: a gift of His joy, a commandment, and a promise.

We have already discussed how we may enter into this gift of joy, by observing Jesus' directives for a happy life.

Jesus' Commandment.

In His last conversation with His disciples, after His resurrection, Jesus gave them (and us) His commandment:

> Go ye therefore, and teach all nations, baptizing them in the name of the Father, and of the Son, and of the Holy Ghost: Teaching them to observe all things whatsoever I have commanded you. (Matt. 28:19-20, KJV)

It is not necessary for us to travel to foreign lands in order to obey this commandment to share in the worldwide ministry of spreading the good news of Jesus. In whatever part of the world we may live, even here in "Christian" America, all around us are lost and lonely souls who do not know the Lord Jesus, who need to hear the good news of God's everlasting love and forgiveness. And it is for this task that Jesus has given us this commandment.

Jesus' Promise.

At the same time that Jesus gave His disciples the commandment, he also gave them an added promise:

> ... And, lo, I am with you alway, even unto the end of the world. (Matt. 28:20, KJV)

Only by accepting Jesus' gift of joy, and depending upon His promise to be with them always, could the little band of disciples have found courage to face the tremendous challenge of His commandment to spread the good news to all the world.

That challenge faces us today. And it is for this task that Jesus has given us His joy, His commandment, and His promise. Praise the Lord!

Part III

Living With Joy Through Various Afflictions

*Rejoice!
In everything give thanks
for this is the will of God
in Christ Jesus concerning
you.*

10

Bible Words About Affliction

In the Old Testament.
The early Hebrews recorded in many places in the Bible their faith in God's power and willingness to come to their aid in all their afflictions.

> ... The LORD hath heard thy affliction. (Gen. 16:11, KJV)

> And when we cried unto the LORD God of our fathers, the LORD heard our voice, and looked on our affliction, and our labour, and our oppression .... (Deut. 26:7, KJV)

When threatened by "a great multitude" Jehoshaphat "sought the Lord" and proclaimed a fast; and stood in the house of the Lord, and prayed:

> ... O LORD God of our fathers, art not thou God in heaven? and rulest not thou over all the kingdoms of the heathen? and in thine hand is there not power and might, so that none is able to withstand thee?
> If, when evil cometh upon us, as the sword, judgment, or pestilence, or famine, we stand before this house, and in thy presence ... and cry unto thee in our affliction, then thou wilt hear and help. (2 Chron. 20:6, 9, KJV)

The Psalmist prayed:

Unto thee, O LORD, do I lift up my soul. O my God, I trust in thee . . .

For thy name's sake, O LORD, pardon my iniquity for it is great.

Turn thee unto me, and have mercy upon me; for I am desolate and afflicted.

Look upon mine affliction and my pain; and forgive all my sins.

O keep my soul and deliver me . . . for I put my trust in thee. (Ps. 25:1, 2, 11, 16, 18, 20, KJV)

"Give thanks to the Lord, because he is good;
   His love is eternal!"
Repeat these words in praise to the Lord,
   all you whom he has saved . . . .
Some wandered in the trackless desert
   and could not find their way to a city to live in;
They were hungry and thirsty and had given up all hope.
Then in their trouble they called to the Lord,
   and he saved them from their distress.
He led them by a straight road to a city where
   they could live.
They must thank the Lord for his constant love,
   for the wonderful thing he did for them . . .
Some were living in gloom and darkness,
   prisoners suffering in chains,
because they had rebelled against the commands
   of Almighty God
   and had rejected his instructions.
They were worn out from hard work;
   they would fall down and no one would help.
Then in their trouble they called to the Lord,
   and he saved them from their distress.
He brought them out of their gloom and darkness
   and broke their chains in pieces.
They must thank the Lord for his constant love,
   for the wonderful things he did for them . . . . (Ps. 107:1-2, 4-18, GNB)

You are a poor specimen if you can't stand the pressure of adversity. (Prov. 24:10, TLB)

Jeremiah addressed God as:

O LORD, my strength, and my fortress, and my refuge in the day of affliction .... (Jer. 16:18, KJV)

The Old Testament writers also recognized God's purposeful use of affliction as a means of perfecting his saints. In Isaiah's prophecy of better times for Israel, God promises not freedom *from* affliction but guidance *through* it:

And though the Lord give you the bread of adversity, and the water of affliction, yet shall not thy teachers be removed into a corner any more, but thine eyes shall see thy teachers:
And thine ears shall hear a word behind thee, saying, This is the way, walk ye in it, when ye turn to the right hand, and when ye turn to the left. (Isa. 30:20-21, KJV)

The Psalmist makes this powerful confession to his God:

Thou hast dealt well with thy servant, O LORD, according unto thy word.
Before I was afflicted I went astray: but now I have kept thy word.
It is good for me that I have been afflicted; that I might learn thy statutes.
I know, O LORD, that thy judgments are right, and that thou in faithfulness hast afflicted me.
Let, I pray thee, thy merciful kindness be for my comfort .... (Ps. 119:65, 67, 71, 75-76, KJV)

"The Gospel According to Job."

No consideration of "affliction" in the Old Testament would be complete without some consideration of the book of Job. This book is one of the most difficult and hard to understand in the Bible—and one of the most profound. In an issue of *The Christian Herald*, Dr. Calvin D. Linton gives an extremely helpful interpretation.

He suggests that the book may be understood "most critically and most crucially" as the "foreshadowing in the Old Testament ... of the Coming One of God."

He says at one point:

> For our part, of course, we who live after the unveiling of the "mystery" of the Cross may understand that through Job God foretells the *vicarious* and *redemptive* suffering, for our salvation, of His Son ... who was ... delivered for our offenses, and was raised again for our "justification" ...
>
> Job received the suffering caused by sin, though he was "perfect," and by his unwavering obedience and faith became the "advocate" of his friends before the throne of God, and prayed for them ....

In the beginning of his trials, Job says:

> ... The Lord gave, and the Lord hath taken away; blessed be the name of the Lord. (Job 1:21, KJV)

Dr. Linton further comments:

> Though far from silent before his accusers (as Jesus was in the perfection of his holiness), Job's faith remained firm. "Though he slay me, yet will I trust him"; "he knoweth the way that I take; when he hath tested me, I shall come forth as gold"; "I know that my redeemer liveth"; "I put on righteousness and it clothed me ...." (Job 13:15; 23:10; 19:25; 29:14)

Dr. Linton concludes his article with these thoughts:

> The fruit of God-ordained affliction, borne faithfully, is glorification ... Job's restoration to an estate greater

than his former, and his public glorification, compose a precise though limited foretelling of the limitless glory which Christ received when he ascended to the Father. . . .

"So the Lord blessed the latter end of Job more than the beginning . . ." (42:12). All in the region saw and acknowledged Job's justification and glorification, and the reason for them. The day will come when all the earth will know, and be required to acknowledge the glory of the Son of Man (Phil. 2:11).

All as dimly but wonderfully foreshadowed in "The Gospel According to Job."

Note: One of the insights that came to me through this article is this: in times of affliction it is not necessary (nor helpful) to torment ourselves with questioning, "Why?" Far better to accept all the bewildering circumstances of our lives unrebelliously, content with the faith that God knows why and it is not necessary for us to understand His reason. Better to put all the power of our hearts and minds on finding the answer to a different question: *"What under these circumstances* is God's will for me?" Not "why?" but "what next?"

In the New Testament.

In the New Testament we find, in addition to the Old Testament insights, a new attitude toward trouble of all kinds, an attitude of *praise and thanksgiving* for affliction.

Jesus described true happiness in the series of statements called the Beatitudes. We have briefly mentioned in a previous chapter the paradoxical character of these famous pronouncements. One of these statements declares:

> Blessed are ye, when men shall revile you, and persecute you, and shall say all manner of evil against you

falsely, for my sake.

Rejoice, and be exceeding glad; for great is your reward in heaven: for so persecuted they the prophets which were before you. (Matt. 5:11-12, KJV)

The Beatitudes and the Ten Commandments.

In a recent sermon,[2] it was pointed out that the Ten Commandments and the Beatitudes are similar in their function and importance, the one in the Old Testament and the other in the New. The Old Testament built its moral structure on the "Law" summarized in the Ten Commandments given through Moses; the New Testament summed up its teachings in the Beatitudes.

The Old Testament "Law" was mostly a series of "Thou shalt not" statements; the New Testament code of life was a series of "Blessed are you, when" declarations. The Old Testament threatened punishment; the New Testament promises rewards. The Old Testament sought to control people by fear; the New Testament is a covenant of love.

Jesus' Life.

Jesus' whole life was given over to the relief of affliction—physical, mental and spiritual. This is so obvious that it is hardly necessary to point out confirming details; but to mention a few of His miracles: The healing of blind Bartimaeus (Mark 10:46), and countless other healings of physical afflictions; the teaching of Nicodemus about being born again (John 3:1-21); the teaching of the "Sermon on the Mount" (Matt. 5-7); the healing of the demoniac (Luke 8:26-40).

Jesus also corrected the then-held view that all calamity was sent as punishment for sin.

Later, as Jesus walked along he saw a man who had been blind from birth.

"Master, whose sin caused this man's blindness," asked the disciples, "his own or his parents'?"

"He was not born blind because of his own sin or that of his parents," returned Jesus, "but to show the power of God at work in him." (John 9:1-3, JBP)

Then Jesus restored the man's sight.

In the Epistles.

Paul emphasized Jesus' attitude toward trouble and affliction of every kind:

> For our light affliction, which is but for a moment, worketh for us a far more exceeding and eternal weight of glory;
>
> While we look not at the things which are seen, but at the things that are not seen: for the things which are seen are temporal; but the things which are not seen are eternal. (2 Cor. 4:17-18, KJV)

The writer of Hebrews sounds a "trumpet call" to all the Christians:

> Remember the days gone by, when, newly enlightened, you met the challenge of great sufferings and held firm. Some of you were abused and tormented to make a public show, while others stood loyally by those who were so treated. For indeed you shared the sufferings of the prisoners, and you cheerfully accepted the seizure of your possessions, knowing that you possessed something better and more lasting . . . . You need endurance, if you are to do God's will and win what he has promised. (Heb. 10:32-37, NEB)

Peter writes to persecuted Christians:

> Awake! be on the alert! Your enemy the devil, like a roaring lion, prowls round looking for someone to devour. Stand up to him, firm in faith, and remember that your

brother Christians are going through the same kinds of suffering while they are in the world. And the God of all grace, who called you into his eternal glory in Christ, will himself, after your brief suffering, restore, establish, and strengthen you on a firm foundation. He holds dominion for ever and ever. Amen. (1 Pet. 5:8-11, NEB)

Thank God, the God and Father of our Lord Jesus Christ, that in his great mercy we have been born again into a life full of hope, through Christ's rising again from the dead! You can now hope for a perfect inheritance beyond the reach of change and decay, "reserved" in Heaven for you. And in the meantime you are guarded by the power of God operating through your faith, till you enter fully into the salvation which is all ready for the dénouement of the last day. This means tremendous joy to you, . . . even though at present you are temporarily harrassed by all kinds of trials and temptations. (1 Pet. 1:3-6, JBP)

11

Living With Joy Through Life's "Afflictions"

Tunnel Experiences.

Some time ago, I was going through a period of discouragement dangerously approaching a depression. In the midst of my struggle to reaffirm "the joy of the Lord" I came across (or was led to?) a brief passage in a book I was reading that proved to be extremely helpful. I have lost track of the book in which I found it, so I am unable to give credit to the author, but the gist of his remarks is found in the following paragraphs.

All of us in the course of our lives have "tunnel experiences," times when the light is obscured, when joy gives place to depression, and we stumble along through the darkness.

Some of these tunnels are short, some of them are long, some seem endless. There are several things about all tunnels that are good to remember, when we find ourselves traveling through one:

1. *Tunnels are never planned nor intended to be permanent residences:* they are designed for us to *go through.*

2. *Tunnels always have two things: an entrance and an exit,* a beginning and an end. (That is what a tunnel is by definition—a way to get from "here" to "there.")

3. *Tunnels are always constructed on the main route.* They are never made on sidings. Life's tunnels too are on the main road; they never wander off into detours.

Tunnels are designed with a purpose; to get us rapidly from where we are to where we are going, avoiding a long and difficult climb over the mountain, or a long detour around it. Life's tunnels have a purpose too. They are to get us from where we are spiritually to where we should be. God is trying to teach us something through every tunnel experience.

We may not always recognize His purpose. It is not necessary that we should. The One who planned and is guiding our pilgrimage knows why this particular tunnel is the best route by which we may get from where we are spiritually to where He wants us to be. *Trust Him!* Later—perhaps much later—you may understand.

4. *The worst thing you can do while traveling through a tunnel is to quit moving, and sit down, and complain!* Keep moving! Remember, every tunnel has an end!

Soon after I discovered this choice advice, I came across another precious bit of wisdom:

> Let your faith, then, "throw its arms around all that God has told you," and in every dark hour remember that "though now for a season, if need be, ye are in heaviness through manifold temptations *it is only like going through a tunnel* [italics mine]. The sun has not ceased shining because the traveler through the tunnel has ceased to see it; and the Sun of Righteousness is still shining although you in your dark tunnel do not see Him. Be patient and trustful, and wait. This time of darkness is only permitted that "the trial of your faith, being much more precious than

of gold that perisheth, though it be tried with fire, might be found unto praise and honor and glory at the appearing of Jesus Christ."[1]

Paul's Ministry of Joy.

No character in the Bible (with the exception of Jesus himself) has such a ministry of joy as does Paul, and that in spite of the fact that from a worldly point of view few people have ever had less reason for "rejoicing" than did he.

In a previous chapter we talked about "sermons without words." Paul, throughout his entire life, marvelously combined the ministry of spoken and written words with the ministry of *being*. He preached repeatedly and forcefully the responsibility of the Christian to *live with joy*. He also preached by what he was.

J.B. Phillips translates Paul's own description of some of his actual experiences like this:

> I have served . . . prison sentences!
> I have been beaten times without number.
> I have faced death again and again.
> I have been beaten the regulation thirty-nine stripes by the Jews five times.
> I have been beaten with rods three times.
> I have been stoned once.
> I have been shipwrecked three times.
> I have been twenty-four hours in the open sea.
> In my travels I have been in constant danger from rivers and floods, from bandits, from my own countrymen, and from pagans. I have faced danger in city streets, danger in the desert, danger on the high seas, danger among false Christians. I have known exhaustion, pain, long vigils, hunger and thirst, doing without meals, cold and lack of clothing. (2 Cor. 11:23-27, JBP)

In his devotional book *For This Day* Phillips comments on this selection:

> Have any of us gone through a tenth of that catalogue of suffering and humiliation? Yet this is the man who can not only say that in all these things we are more than conquerors, but can also "reckon that the sufferings of this present time are not worthy to be compared with the glory which shall be revealed to us" (Romans 8:18).
>
> Here is no arm-chair philosopher, no ivory-tower scholar, but a man of almost incredible drive and courage, living out in actual human dangers and agonies the implications of his unswerving faith.[2]

This is also the same man who in another letter wrote these inspiring words:

> As cooperators with God himself we beg you, then, not to fail to use the grace of God.
>
> ... We want to prove ourselves genuine ministers of God whatever we have to go through—patient endurance of troubles or even disasters, being flogged or imprisoned; being mobbed, having to work like slaves, having to go without food or sleep. All this we want to meet with sincerity, with insight and patience; by sheer kindness and the Holy Spirit; with genuine love, speaking the plain truth, and living by the power of God. Our sole defense, our only weapon, is a life of integrity, whether we meet honor or dishonor, praise or blame.... Never far from death, yet here we are alive, always "going through it" yet never "going under." We know sorrow, yet our joy is inextinguishable. We have "nothing to bless ourselves with," yet we bless many others with true riches. We are penniless, and yet in reality we have everything worth having. (2 Cor. 6:1-11, JBP)

Give Thanks!

> In every thing give thanks: for this is the will of God in Christ Jesus concerning you. (2 Thess. 5:18, KJV)

"Natural man" rejects this directive as utter nonsense! Give thanks in everything? In all kinds of bitter afflictions? In loneliness? In bereavement? In physical handicaps? In sickness and suffering? Give thanks in and for these bitter experiences? How absurd!

And yet there is no other possible interpretation of the Bible teachings.

Of Thankfulness.

> Fill us with thy Spirit so that we may give thanks always for all things unto thee, our Father, in the name of our Lord Jesus Christ. (See Eph. 5:18-20.)

The prayer of thankfulness seems at first to present the least difficulty to the beginning pray-er. How easy it is in quiet times of peace and joy to lift the heart in gratitude to the Source of all our blessings! But this is only the first step in learning to live life in a constant, unwavering spirit of thankfulness . . . .

How sadly we recognize in ourselves the tendency to be grateful only for those things which bring us momentary satisfaction, and how slowly we learn to "give thanks always for all things."

The Sand in the Oyster.

> Theoretically, we recognize the truth symbolized by the sand in the oyster: it is the minute grain of sand within the shell, unwelcome and irritating, which produces in the course of time the lustrous, perfect pearl. So in our lives, as we look back over the years, we can see the precious values that have come out of the very trials and tribulations through which we so reluctantly passed—the illnesses, the disappointments, the economic crises, the family estrangements, the failures, the disloyalty of a trusted friend—all the long list of woes. But it is one thing

to look back to past trials, and recognize thankfully blessings that have come as a result of them, but it is quite a different thing to thank God in the midst of them.

And yet, should we not in fact, be thankful for those tragic experiences which teach us what is needful for the salvation of our souls? For those which, accepted as from God's hand, develop in us those Christlike qualities, for the growth of which all life seems to be designed? For those which force on us the recognition of our complete dependence on God's love and awaken in us the realization of His complete sufficiency to meet every need?

What amazing new depths of joyous living are available to us when we achieve this much-to-be-desired ability "to give thanks to God always for all things"—to accept life in its totality from God's hands, and to thank Him for *life*—its joys, its sorrows, its triumphs, its failures, its evil and its good—to praise God in the midst of it, as the continuing Creator and Sustainer of our very being![3]

The Joy of The Christian Religion.

In his book *Love Is a Spendthrift*,[4] Paul Scherer has some lovely insights into the joy of the Christian religion:

1

The fundamental joy of the Christian religion isn't in living a good life. I can imagine getting tired of that! The fundamental joy of it is in standing with God against some darkness or some void and watching the light come.[5]

2

In suffering and in sorrow, in failure and in despair, there is One whose presence is a melody in the heart, and His very will a song .... Paul, in prison, writes to the Philippians, "Rejoice in the Lord alway: and again I say Rejoice!" and wins an empire for Christ. Such songs in the night are the cradlesongs of every victory that God has wrought.[6]

3

Religion is like riding a bicycle: the only safety there is lies in riding! Otherwise you can't even stay on. Momentum is the secret of poise. You'll spend all the days of your pilgrimage being upset, until you learn to fling yourself on such faith as you have, and instead of trying to put up with the wrongs people do you, swing out to set them right![7]

4

Joy surprises you in that place beyond the self and all of its business where you quit supposing that things have to go as you like, calling it a problem for faith when they don't. "Why should this happen to me?" Let me put you a tougher one: "Why shouldn't it happen to you?" You remember what happened to Paul and to Jesus before him. Joy can never surprise you until you quit tempting the God you have to be the God you want, and begin allowing him, as far as you are concerned, to be God on His own terms.[8]

Worth While

It is easy enough to be pleasant
   When life flows by like a song,
But the man worth while is the man who can smile
   When everything goes dead wrong.

For the test of the heart is trouble,
   And it always comes with the years,
And the smile that is worth the praises of earth
   Is the smile that shines through tears.[9]

Corrie and Betsie.

(Probably most of you reading this book are already familiar with the story below, a true story from Corrie ten Boom's *The Hiding Place.* But I have included it here because it is the most forceful confirmation I have come across of the amazing wisdom of Paul's directive: "In every thing give thanks.")

The apostles were not the only ones whose joy was put to the test in prisons! Corrie ten Boom describes in detail many of the trials she and her sister Betsie endured in the German concentration camp of Ravensbruck, where they were imprisoned because they had befriended Jews. They were assigned to a barracks, a long, gray building. They entered a large room where two hundred or more women were at work, knitting socks. On either side were two still larger units. Corrie tells what happened next:

> Betsie and I followed a prison guard through the door at the right ... The place was filthy.... As our eyes adjusted to the gloom we saw that there were no individual beds at all, but great square piers stacked three high, and wedged side by side and end to end with only an occasional aisle slicing through.
>
> We followed our guide.... At last she pointed to a second tier in the center of a large block. To reach it we had to stand on the bottom level, and haul ourselves up, and then crawl across three other straw-filled platforms to reach the one that we would share with—how many? We lay back, struggling against the nausea that swept over us from the reeking straw.
>
> Suddenly I sat up, striking my head on the cross slats above. Something had pinched my leg.
>
> "Fleas!" I cried. "Betsie, the place is swarming with them!"
>
> We scrambled across the intervening platforms, heads low to avoid another bump, dropped down to the aisle, and wedged our way to a patch of light.
>
> "Here! And here another one!" I wailed. "Betsie, how can we live in such a place!"
>
> "Show us. Show us how." It was said so matter of factly it took me a second to realize she was praying. More and more the distinction between prayer and the rest of life seemed to be vanishing for Betsie.

"Corrie!" she said excitedly. "He's given us the answer! Before we asked, as He always does! In the Bible this morning. Where was it? Read that part again!"

I glanced down the long dim aisle to make sure no guard was in sight, then drew the Bible from its pouch. "It was in First Thessalonians," I said.... In the feeble light I turned the pages. "Here it is: 'Comfort the frightened, help the weak, be patient with everyone. See that none of you repays evil for evil, but always seek to do good to one another and to all....' " It seemed written expressly to Ravensbruck.

"Go on," said Betsie. "That wasn't all."

"Oh yes: '... to one another and to all. Rejoice always, pray constantly, give thanks in all circumstances; for this is the will of God in Christ Jesus—' "

"That's it, Corrie! That's His answer. 'Give thanks in all circumstances!' That's what we can do. We can start right now to thank God for every single thing about this new barracks!"

I stared at her, then around me at the dark, foul-aired room.

"Such as?" I asked.

"Such as being assigned here together."

I bit my lip. "Oh yes, Lord Jesus!"

"Such as what you're holding in your hands."

I looked down at the Bible. "Yes! Thank You, dear Lord, that there was no inspection when we entered here! Thank You for all the women, here in this room, who will meet You in these pages."

"Yes," said Betsie. "Thank You for the very crowding here. Since we're packed so close, that many more will hear!" She looked at me expectantly. "Corrie!" she prodded.

"Oh, all right. Thank You for the jammed, crammed, stuffed, packed, suffocating crowds."

"Thank You," Betsie went on serenely, "for the fleas and for—"

The fleas! This was too much. "Betsie, there's no way even God can make me grateful for a flea."

" 'Give thanks in *all* circumstances,' " she quoted. "It doesn't say 'in pleasant circumstances.' Fleas are part of this place where God has put us."

And so we stood between piers of bunks and gave thanks for fleas. But this time I was sure Betsie was wrong.[10]

The weeks dragged by. Betsie was finally assigned to a knitting job with a group of workers in the dormitory. She was a fast knitter and completed her quota of socks early in the day. There was practically no supervision of the group in the dormitory, and Betsie spent much of the time reading the Bible and ministering to the other prisoners. Corrie goes on:

One evening I got back to the barracks late from a wood-gathering foray outside the walls.... Betsie was waiting for me, as always, so that we could wait through the food line together. Her eyes were twinkling.

"You're looking extraordinarily pleased with yourself," I told her.

"You know we've never understood why we had so much freedom in the big room," she said. "Well—I've found out."

That afternoon, she said, there'd been confusion in her knitting group about sock sizes and they'd asked the supervisor to come and settle it.

"But she wouldn't. She wouldn't step through the door and neither would the guards. And you know why?"

Betsie could not keep the triumph from her voice: "Because of the fleas! That's what she said, 'That place is crawling with fleas!' "

My mind rushed back to our first hour in this place. I remembered Betsie's bowed head, remembered her thanks to God for creatures I could see no use for.

God's Canary.

Madame Guyon looked upon her cell in the French prison as a cage, God's cage, and she saw herself as God's canary, placed there by the Lord to sing for his delight. So she wrote her sweetest songs and sang her most moving melodies in France's great prisons, bound there for the sake of her faith in Jesus, and praised God for putting her there in his cage to sing for him.[12]

Another Singing Prisoner.

... About midnight Paul and Silas were praying and singing hymns to God while the other prisoners were listening to them. Suddenly there was a great earthquake, big enough to shake the foundations of the prison. Immediately all the doors flew open and everyone's chains were unfastened. When the jailer woke and saw that the doors of the prison had been opened he drew his sword and was on the point of killing himself, for he imagined that all the prisoners had escaped. But Paul called out to him at the top of his voice,

"Don't hurt yourself—we are all here!"

Then the jailer called for lights, rushed in, and trembling all over, fell at the feet of Paul and Silas. He led them outside, and said,

"Sirs, what must I do to be saved?"

And they replied,

"Believe in the Lord Jesus and then you will be saved, you and your household."

Then they told him and all the members of his household the message of God. There and then in the middle of the night he took them aside and washed their wounds, and he himself and all his family were baptized without delay. Then he took them into his house and offered them food, he and his whole household overjoyed at finding faith in God. (Acts 16:25-35, JBP)

Whate'er My God Ordains Is Right

Whate'er my God ordains is right;
   His holy will abideth;
I will be still, whate'er He doth
   And follow where He guideth.
He is my God; though dark my road,
   He holds me that I shall not fall;
   Wherefore to Him I leave it all.

Whate'er my God ordains is right;
   He never will deceive me;
He leads me by the proper path;
   I know He will not leave me.
I take content what He has sent
   His hand can turn my griefs away,
   And patiently I wait His day.

Whate'er my God ordains is right;
   Here shall my stand be taken.
Though sorrow, need, or death be mine,
   Yet am I not forsaken.
My Father's care is round me there;
   He holds me that I shall not fall.
   And so to Him I leave it all.[13]

A Final Word from Paul: "Always Be Joyful, Always Be Thankful"

   Dear brothers, warn those who are lazy; comfort those who are frightened; take tender care of those who are weak; and be patient with everyone. See that no one pays back evil for evil, but always try to do good to each other and to everyone else. Always be joyful. Always keep on praying. No matter what happens, always be thankful, for this is God's will for you who belong to Christ Jesus. (1 Thess. 5:14-18, TLB)

12

Some Common Obstacles To Living With Joy

In considering life's tunnel experiences we recognized that in every one of them, God has a purpose for us. He is trying to teach us something through each particular experience. He is constantly drawing us to himself, seeking to strengthen our faith to enable each of us to accept His joy. We turn now to consider some of the common obstacles which often prevent us from living with joy.

1. *Lack of Faith.*
The chief obstacle is our lack of faith. If we really "believed our beliefs" we should find upwelling in our hearts the same steady, undefeatable joy that enabled the early Christians to meet victoriously every difficult and tragic situation, not only courageously but even joyfully.

The Faith of the Martyrs.
The history of the birth of Christianity is filled with true accounts of the joyous faith of these early Christians in the face of sufferings of all kinds, even in martyrdom. Stephen was the first of a long line of martyrs. His

story is told in Acts 6 and 7. Of Stephen's martyrdom, Watchman Nee has written:

> But he, [Stephen] being full of the Holy Ghost, looked up stedfastly into heaven, and saw the glory of God, and Jesus standing on the right hand of God . . . (Acts 7:55, KJV). Stephen's first words to the council were of God and His glory. "Men, brethren and fathers, hearken," he said. "The God of glory appeared unto our father Abraham. . . ." The man who sees that glory knows he must respond. He cannot do otherwise. Abraham responded, and through all the setbacks and discouragements of his pilgrimage the vision of God's glory carried him in triumph . . . . Stephen set out first of all to remind his hearers of this.
>
> They heard Stephen's testimony and rejected it, only to become suddenly aware that he himself was beholding that of which he spoke! Full of the Holy Ghost, he looked up steadfastly "and saw the glory of God." He who appeared to Abraham and He whom Stephen saw were one and the same. There is no change in Him. And that same God, His splendour still undimmed, now carried Stephen through his own terrible crisis. What matters an extra stone or two to one who beholds the glory of God?[1]

Joy in Their Hearts.

The martyrs went to their deaths in the arena or at the stake with songs on their lips and joy in their hearts sustained by the faith that they were doing God's will and that through suffering the coming of His Kingdom would be hastened. When entreated by the Roman proconsul to save his own life by offering incense to Caesar as deity, the aged Polycarp, last of those who were personally acquainted with the twelve disciples, answered: "Eighty and six years have I served Him and He did me no wrong. How can I blaspheme my King, that saved me?" And as the flames consumed his flesh, he prayed: "I bless Thee that Thou didst deem me worthy of this day and hour."[2]

For All the Saints.

> For all the saints who from their labors rest,
> Who Thee by faith before the world confessed,
> Thy name, O Jesus, be forever blest:
> > Alleluia! Alleluia!
>
> Thou wast their Rock, their Fortress and their Might,
> Thou, Lord, their captain in the well-fought fight,
> And Thou, in darkness drear, their one true light:
> > Alleluia! Alleluia!
>
> O blest communion, fellowship divine!
> We feebly struggle, they in glory shine;
> Yet all are one in Thee, for all are Thine:
> > Alleluia! Alleluia! . . .[3]

Self-centeredness.

Lack of faith often grows out of an exaggerated self-centeredness. In his book *Fresh Every Morning*, Gerald Kennedy has a chapter entitled "In the Name of the Lord" which is a commentary on the biblical story of David and Goliath, from which the following excerpts are reprinted:

> Goliath was more amused than angry (when he saw the lad who had accepted his challenge) and he cursed the shepherd boy. Then David replied, "You come to me with a sword and with a spear and with a javelin; but I come to you in the name of the Lord of Hosts, the God of the armies of Israel, whom you have defied." Fitting a stone in his sling, he threw it at Goliath, pierced his forehead and killed him. What I want us to think about for a little while is the great affirmation of David: "I come to you in the name of the Lord of hosts."
>
> Let us begin with the observation that GOODNESS ALWAYS SEEMS WEAKER THAN EVIL . . . Through nineteen centuries the Church has been David against the Goliath of the world. People seldom

take it very seriously.... Yet Hitler was not the first dictator and in all probability will not be the last to be surprised by the strength of the Church which has seemed so weak. For when the crisis comes, there has been an unseen spiritual power possessed by the Church which has brought down tyranny....

Every change in society for the good has been against an enemy that seemed invincible....

Another truth that comes from this story is that

MAN IS NOT SELF-SUFFICIENT

The strength of Goliath was only in himself, and his pride betrayed him. David proclaimed that he came in the name of a mighty faith....

We have learned much about the workings of the human mind through psychiatry. There is, however, one fundamental weakness which needs to be noticed.... It must be said that much psychology assumes that man's problems can be solved from within himself and through his own wisdom. It assumes that man is self-sufficient and that by proper adjustment he can live happily and successfully. With this point of view religion finds no agreement....

A Scottish shepherd one time said that sheep caught in a blizzard can live for seven or eight days by eating their own wool. But at the end of that time they will freeze to death. That, my brethren, is a parable. We can feed upon ourselves and be concerned only with ourselves for a time, but there is no lasting answer in that process. Goliath represents those who glory in their own strength and their own success but discover finally that it does not save them.

Finally let us note that there is

POWER IN RELIGIOUS FAITH

For two thousand years we have been using the phrase "In the name of Jesus Christ".... In that confession is the strength of each Christian....

There is a name that is power and victory and joy. It is Jesus Christ.[4]

Without Faith.
The writer of Hebrews in his famous chapter on faith, says:

> ... Without faith it is impossible to please him: [God] for he that cometh to God must believe that he is .... (Heb. 11:6, KJV)

I never read this verse without remembering an incident that took place several years ago in an adult education class that I was leading. We were spending a number of sessions on prayer. I have forgotten exactly how it came into the discussion, but someone read this verse aloud.

Suddenly, a woman broke into the conversation, obviously much agitated. "That's only partly true," she exclaimed. "I know! Recently my daughter had her first baby, and he was born blind! I was devastated! I was in agony! And I tried to pray. But all I could say was: 'God—if there is a God—help me!'"

She paused, and the group sat in stunned silence, deeply moved. Then the woman went on, very quietly, in a voice that was full of awe. "And He did," she said. "He honored even that prayer! He eased my agony!"

Your Faith.
If you recognize that *your* faith is weak, there is a clear path to follow in the Bible teaching:

> *Saturate yourself with the Word of God.* (Faith comes by hearing and hearing by the Word of God.)
> *Take advantage of opportunities to hear inspired teaching, and participate in Spirit-led worship.*
> *Associate yourself with a Spirit-filled fellowship.*
> *"Pray without ceasing!"*

13

Some Common Obstacles To Living With Joy (Continued)

In the previous chapter we recognized a *lack of faith* as the chief obstacle to living with joy during the tunnel experiences of our lives.

Depression.
This is due to the fact that a lack of faith opens us up to spells of mental and spiritual depression. This is by far the most common affliction that interferes with our joy of all the tunnels we travel through. None other seems so difficult to control, so persistently recurring, so devastating in its effects upon us and upon those around us. Moreover, I am sure it is a universal experience. No one entirely escapes it.

Some people, however, learn how to pass through the tunnel rapidly, so that the time spent in the darkness is greatly shortened; whereas some seem to linger, deliberately prolonging the time of darkness. Perhaps these are the people Rebecca McCann had in mind when she put these words into the mouth of her "cheerful cherub":

> The members of our human race
>   Who move me most to scornful diction
> Are sensitive and injured souls,
>   Luxuriating in affliction.[1]

Depression seems to be caused by innumerable and varied circumstances—ill health, financial troubles, disappointments, failures, unjust treatment, bereavement—each individual could probably add to the list.

And yet the infinite variety of "reasons" for depression can be summed up in one all-inclusive cause: self-centeredness. Once again Rebecca McCann has expressed a tremendous truth in one of her rhymes:

> Whenever I am gloomy
>   In time I come to see
> It's just because I'm thinking
>   Entirely of me.[2]

If this is true, (and it seems to me that honest facing of instances when depression has held us in its grip, will confirm it), if self-centeredness is the basic cause of depression, then recognizing this gives us needful guidance as to how to overcome it.

Just as trying to be happy never works—just as happiness is a by-product of focusing on "those good and satisfying things which produce happiness"—so depression will never be overcome by fighting *against it*. The only cure comes from dethroning Self as the center of life, and recentering our whole life—our thoughts, our aims, our actions—on God himself.

And so once again we are brought back to Jesus and His teachings. No matter what the circumstances are that have caused our depression, the way to overcome it is the same: to follow the clear directives of Jesus which will inevitably produce joy, and drive out depression.

This is the kind of rejoicing that the prophet is claiming in the following passage:

> Although the fig tree may not blossom,
> nor fruit be on the vines,
> the produce of the olive fail
> and the field yield no food,
> the flock be cut off from the fold,
> and there be no herd in the stalls,
> yet I will rejoice in the Lord,
> I will joy in the God of my salvation.
> The Lord God is my strength;
> He makes my feet like hinds' feet,
> He makes me tread upon my high places.
> (Habakkuk 3:17-19)

We may not be concerned about fig trees and grape vines, or flocks or herds, but we can each rewrite the "althoughs" to fit our situation, *and then* make our own joyous declaration:

> Yet will I rejoice in the Lord—
> I will joy in the God of my salvation
> The Lord God is my strength.

A Personal Confession.
During the months of assembling the materials for this book, I suddenly found myself plunged into the worst depression I had known in years.

The immediate cause was the death of a dearly loved sister, Lilla, or rather the circumstances surrounding her death. She was eighty-nine, almost three years older than I, the last living member besides myself of the family in which we grew up. Her last few weeks were miserably unhappy, pain-wracked, and filled with bitterness and rebellion. Her mind was hopelessly confused, and the last time I saw her in a nursing home, after an intestinal operation, she did not even recognize me.

My distress over her condition was so keen that my daughter and her husband, with whom I have lived for the last twenty years, immediately began to explore the possibility of moving her from New Jersey, halfway across the country, to care for her in our home in Columbus, Ohio.

My heart was filled with gratitude and thanksgiving. But it took some time to work out all the necessary arrangements, and when all the difficulties had been solved and we were ready to set a definite date for the move, the news of her death brought all our plans to a sudden, jolting conclusion.

When the news reached me, my first reaction was of relief, that at last she was released from her worn-out body; and I drew comfort from the biblical assurance that "to be absent from the body is to be present with the Lord." But my first reaction was followed by a wave of disappointment and depression for which I was totally unprepared.

For a number of days I fought desperately and unsuccessfully with my feelings. I put aside my uncompleted manuscript with a guilty recognition that I was in no condition to write about "living with joy," and added to my depression a sense of ignominious failure.

And then, early one morning, I woke up to face another grim day. My eyes fell on the cloth banner on my wall: "This is the day which the Lord hath made; we will rejoice and be glad in it" (Ps. 118:24, KJV).

I read the words to myself somberly, with no slightest response of my spirit. I was very far from "rejoicing and being glad."

And then the Lord brought to my mind the words of Andrew Murray: "He that seeks gladness shall not find it; He that seeks the Lord and His will shall find gladness unsought."[3]

And my spirit within me witnessed to the truth of these words! I was *not* seeking God's will, but was rebelling against it. It was obviously *not* God's will that I should have the anticipated joy of caring for Lilla in her final illness. My depression was due, not to her death, but to my refusal to accept God's will in the situation. It was useless to mourn over what could not be changed. It was useless to ask "Why?" What was needed on my part was complete trust that God *had* a reason, and that His decision was for the best good of all concerned. Not "Why?" but "What next?" was the important question.

And in the light of that revelation I confessed to God my sin of rebellious self-centeredness, and asked His forgiveness. Then I rose and faced the day, not yet with joy, but with an acceptance of His will, and a peace that I knew was the foretaste of joy to come.

The Power to Live By.
(The following quotation is relevant at this point.)

> Is there anyone or anything who can say to us *Come unto me* and I will satisfy you? I will restore you, I will give you rest, the power to live by? It cannot possibly be science. There is no discount to what science has done. It has enlarged the range of our thought of the universe. It has increased the comforts of life and living. But! All its paths lead up to boundaries where its researches end and the things we most profoundly *want* lie beyond those boundaries. Until science can learn how *to ennoble the soul, and give it over-brimming joy in life*, it cannot be an alternative to Christ....
>
> Quakerism was born in the discovery that there is no alternative. "When all my hopes... in all men were gone," George Fox said, "so that I had nothing outwardly

to help me, nor could I tell what to do, then, Oh, then I heard a voice which said, 'There is one, even Christ Jesus, that can speak to thy condition.' "[4]

The One Necessity.

In his book *Fresh Every Morning*, Gerald Kennedy says:

> I know a great deal about the assorted darknesses and depressions that can afflict the human spirit. And I know very well indeed how faith in oneself and one's own integrity, let alone faith in an omnipotent God, can be severely shaken and tested.
>
> Of one thing I am quite certain. There is nothing that can help a man through a lengthy period of recovery better than a sustained faith in God, whatever one's feelings happen to be.
>
> I have read a great deal during the last few years, but I have never discovered anything that even remotely helps those who have to endure such times of depression unless it be found in, or derived from, the teachings of Jesus Christ and the New Testament generally.[5]

Count Your Blessings.

(The words of this old hymn are still good advice for those who are struggling against depression.)

When upon life's billows you are tempest-tossed,
When you are discouraged thinking all is lost,
Count your many blessings, name them one by one,
And it will surprise you what the Lord has done.

Are you overburdened with a load of care?
Does the cross seem heavy you are called to bear?
Count your many blessings, every doubt will fly,
And you will be singing as the days go by.

So amid the conflict, whether great or small,
Do not be discouraged, God is over all . . . .
Count your many blessings, name them one by one,
Then give thanks to God for all that He has done.[6]

Summary: Put God First.

Self-centeredness can be overcome in one way and in one way only—by focusing your entire life on God. Jesus' first commandment is the complete answer to self-centeredness:

> ... Thou shalt love the Lord thy God with all thy heart, and with all thy soul, and with all thy mind. (Matt. 22:37, KJV)

And in Proverbs the same truth is stated in this way:

> In everything you do, put God first, and he will direct you and crown your efforts with success. (Prov. 3:6, TLB)

In this effort to seek and find God and His will for our lives, we know we can rely upon His promise (through Jeremiah):

> And ye shall seek me, and find me, when ye shall search for me with all your heart. And I will be found of you, saith the LORD . . . . (Jer. 29:13-14, KJV)

A Prayer for All Conditions of Men

O God, the Creator and Preserver of all mankind, we humbly beseech thee for all sorts and conditions of men; that thou wouldest be pleased to make thy ways known unto them, thy saving health unto all nations.

More especially we pray for thy holy Church universal; that it may be so guided and governed by thy good Spirit, that all who profess and call themselves Christians may be led into the way of truth, and hold the faith in unity of spirit, in the bond of peace, and in righteousness of life.

Finally, we commend to thy fatherly goodness all those who are any ways afflicted, or distressed in mind, body, or estate; that it may please thee to comfort and relieve them, according to their several necessities; giving them patience under their sufferings, and a happy issue out of all their afflictions. And this we beg for Jesus Christ's sake. Amen.[2]

14

Some Common Obstacles To Living With Joy (Continued)

We have considered the most important obstacle to joyous living, our lack of faith, and consequent openness to spells of depression. We turn our attention now to a second important obstacle.

2. *A Guilty Conscience.*
Probably few factors in our lives block the experience of joy as effectively as a guilty conscience. The memories of past sins—both of commission and of omission—cast the gloomiest of shadows over our lives. Often a deepening relationship with God increases our awareness of our own sinfulness.

That was true of Isaiah. When in the Temple he caught a vision of God's holiness, his response was utter dejection because of his own unworthiness!

> Woe is me, for I am ruined!
> Because I am a man of unclean lips,
> And I live among a people of unclean lips;
> For my eyes have seen the King, the Lord of hosts. (Isa. 6:5, NAS)

Guilt carries with it a train of unpleasant consequences. It distorts our understanding of everything that happens. It produces discouragement, lack of self-esteem, moodiness.

The Pilgrim's Progress.
In the third chapter of John Bunyan's famous allegory, he writes:

> Now I saw in my dream that the highway up which Christian was to go was fenced on either side with a wall that was called 'Salvation' (Isa. 26:1). Up this way, therefore, did burdened Christian run, but not without great difficulty, because of the load on his back.
>
> He ran thus till he came to a place somewhat ascending; and upon that place stood a cross, and a little below, in the bottom, a sepulchre. So I saw in my dream, that just as Christian came up with the cross, his burden loosed from off his shoulders, and fell from off his back, and began to tumble, and so continued to do till it came to the mouth of the sepulchre, where it fell in, and I saw it no more.

When God releases us of our guilt and burden, we are as those that leap for joy.

> Then was Christian glad and lightsome, and said with a merry heart, "He hath given me rest by His sorrow, and life by His Death." Then he stood still awhile to look and wonder; for it was very surprising to him that the sight of the cross should thus ease him of his burden. He looked, therefore, and looked again, even till the springs that were in his head sent the water down his cheeks (Zech. 12:10). Now, as he stood looking and weeping, behold, three Shining Ones came to him, and saluted him with "Peace be to thee." So the first said to him, "Thy sins be forgiven thee" (Mark 2:5); the second stripped him of his rags, and clothed him with a change of raiment (Zech. 3:4); the third also set a mark on his forehead (Eph. 1:13),

and gave him a roll with a seal upon it, which he bade him look on as he ran, and that he should give it in at the celestial gate; so they went their way. Then Christian gave three leaps for joy, and went on, singing:

"Thus far I did come, laden with my sin;
Nor could aught ease the grief that I was in,
Till I came hither: what a place is this!
Must here be the beginning of my bliss?
Must here the burden fall from off my back?
Must here the strings that bound it to me crack?
Blest cross! blest sepulchre! blest rather be
The Man that was there put to shame for me!"

Our Need For Forgiveness.

No joy can come to us when we are carrying a burden of guilt. But no one need carry *that* burden. The Bible gives us frequent and complete instructions on how to get rid of it.

In Acts, Peter says to the crowding people:

Repent ye . . . that your sins may be blotted out, when the times of refreshing shall come from the presence of the Lord . . . . (Acts 3:19, KJV)

When we truly repent, God's forgiveness is freely given, (provided that we also forgive others). The "times of refreshing" when we have the comforting assurance of God's forgiveness come from the awareness of God's presence surrounding us everywhere.

Forgiving ourselves is also a necessary part of God's healing process.

Peter and Paul.[1]

God's forgiveness is to be had for the asking, but genuine acceptance of forgiveness is sometimes difficult to achieve. Wallowing in a sense of our own unworthiness can do nothing toward rectifying the evil already committed nor toward preventing its recurrence. The proof of true repentance is the ability to accept forgiveness (to forgive oneself) and to face life again renewed, courageous and joyous.

How the course of history would have been changed had two of the early Christians (Peter and Paul) refused to accept God's forgiveness, and remained self-condemnatory all the rest of their lives!

Consider Peter. On the fateful night of Jesus' arrest, what a coward he turned out to be! After he had "followed afar off," he finally sat down among a crowd in the hall of the high priest's house, where Jesus had been taken. A maid noticed him.

Maid: This man also was with him.

Peter: Woman, I know him not.

Later:

Man: Thou art also one of them.

Peter: Man, I am not.

And still later:

Man: Of a truth this fellow also was with him: for he is a Galilaean.

Peter: Man, I know not what thou sayest. (Luke 22:56-60, KJV)

No wonder, moments later, when his eyes met those of Jesus, that Peter "went out and wept bitterly." Eventually, however, Peter was able to accept God's forgiveness, and to forgive himself, although surely he could never forget completely his denial of his Master. He did, however, find strength to go forward to years of faithful service to his beloved Lord, and to probable triumphant martyrdom.

And consider Paul. He was another man who had good reason to be crushed under a hopeless load of guilt and remorse because of his bitter persecution of the followers of Jesus in Jerusalem. In Acts 9:1 he is described as "breathing out threatenings and slaughter" against the disciples of the Lord. Yet it was this same Paul after his conversion, who testified before Agrippa:

> I once thought it my duty to oppose with the utmost vigor the name of Jesus of Nazareth. Yes, that is what I did in Jerusalem, and I had many of God's people imprisoned on the authority of the chief priests, and when they were on trial for their lives I gave my vote against them. Many and many a time in all the synagogues I had them punished and I used to try to force them to deny their Lord. I was mad with fury against them, and I hounded them to distant cities. (Acts 26:9-11, JBP)

Paul goes on to describe his experience on the road to Damascus, and concludes his speech as follows:

> After that, King Agrippa, I could not disobey the heavenly vision. But both in Damascus and in Jerusalem, through the whole of Judaea, and to the gentiles, I preached that men should repent and turn to God and live lives to prove their change of heart. This is why the Jews seized me in the Temple and tried to kill me. To this day I have received help from God himself, and I stand here as a witness to high and low, adding nothing to what the prophets and Moses foretold should take place, that is, that Christ should suffer, that he should be the first to rise from the dead, and so proclaim the message of light both to our people and to the gentiles! (Acts 26:19-23, JBP)

A False Self-Consciousness.

Augustus and J.C. Hare have written the following:

> ... We are not to spend our days in watching our own vices, in gazing at our own sins, in stirring and raking up

all the mud of our past lives; but to lift our thoughts from our own corrupt nature to Him who put on that nature in order to deliver it from corruption, and to fix our contemplation and our affections on Him who came to clothe us in His perfect righteousness, and through whom and in whom, if we are united to Him by a living faith, we too become righteous. Thus, like the Apostle, we are to forget that which is behind, and to keep our eyes bent on the prize of our high calling, to which we are to press onward, and which we may attain in Christ Jesus . . . .

. . . In the Christian view of men, no less than in the natural, the healthy normal state is not the subjective, but the objective, that in which, losing his own individual life, he finds it again in Christ, that in which he does not make himself the object of his contemplation and action, but directs them both steadily and continually toward the will and glory of God.[2]

How To Live Like a King's Kid.

In Harold Hill's delightful book *How to Live Like a King's Kid* (South Plainfield, N.J.: Bridge Publishing, 1974) the final chapter includes a moving story of how to deal with a guilty conscience. The following excerpts are included here by permission.

Not long after I began to believe, and after I had received the Baptism in the Holy Spirit, I was complaining because God wasn't using my ministry in a more powerful way. When I asked Him to show me what the trouble was, He showed me the passage in Matthew where Jesus said that if you bring your gift to the altar and remember that your brother has something against you, you have to leave your gift and go and be reconciled to the brother before you can give your gift to God.

I knew there was a broken relationship that had to be taken care of in my life. And that mess I had made was fogging my signals, fouling up my receiving apparatus. I couldn't hear what God was saying, because I was broadcasting so much static of my own.

One morning, in a drunken stupor—before I was saved—I had gotten out of bed in terrible shape—as usual—and I saw a doctor bill lying on my dresser. It was bad timing. My wife should not have put it there. But I opened it, and I resented it. I got on the phone and told the doctor how many shysters I thought he was, and I said a lot of other things, none of which were complimentary to him or his profession. I really told him off, finishing with, "If you live to be a thousand years old and me ten thousand, I'm never going to pay you that bill—" And I slammed down the phone, burning my bridges behind me.

Time went on. I got saved. Met Jesus. Began to walk this life in the Spirit.

The doctor lived only five or six houses away on a one-way street. I couldn't go anywhere without passing his house. Across the street was a vacant lot, and I'd turn my head and look at the weedy vacant lot. I actually got a northbound crick in my neck from looking that way every time. I didn't want to see the doctor if he happened to be outside, because he bugged me. I didn't want to face the fact that I had behaved like a real pagan with him. I had brought this thing on myself, but I tried to rationalize.

When the Lord showed me the Scripture, I said, "Well, Lord, that's a misprint. He ought to come to me. I'm the injured one. Besides, that's all in the past, water over the dam. Won't do any good to re-open the discussion." But no matter how much I rationalized, God didn't change the Scripture to conform to my way of thinking, and I got more and more miserable.

One night, I was so heavy with guilt, all I could think of was that doctor's name. God brought him to my attention every time I tried to pray. I was dying on the vine spiritually. When you bring your gifts to the altar, when you come in the attitude of prayer and worship, the first name that comes into your head of somebody who bugs you, is your upper most problem, blocking the kingdom of heaven from coming into evidence in your own life. Awareness of a roadblock brings responsibility to do something about it.

And so one night I was so heavy with guilt, I said, "All right, Lord, I'll go. By Your grace, I'm going to his house and make it right." And I walked past those five houses, like fifty miles. It was too short a run to drive it; I had to walk up, and I knew all the neighbors were looking at me and saying, "There goes the guilty one."

I was so conscious of this guilt that I was sure everyone was whispering, "There goes the sinner. He's going up and confess."

And Satan was throwing everything in the book at me. "You don't want to go and apologize to him. You don't have to."

"Of course, I don't have to," I agreed with him! "I can die and not apologize. I have a choice of drying up. I have a choice of no answered prayer. Oh, I've got a lot of choices, but they're second, and third, and fourth hand. They're not the best ones. King's kids want first best. And God wants me to have first best, but I'll not get it except God's way."

I knocked on the door, no answer. I heaved a big sigh of relief and slunk back home. It took me several weeks to muster up enough courage and scrape up enough grace to go back the second time. This time his wife answered the door and said, "The doctor's not at home."

The third time, on the way up the walk, I prayed, "Lord, I'm going, but You're going to have to do the doing."

I knocked on his door again. And when he opened the door that day, I shivered. He was several inches taller than I am, and he looked down on me as if I was an annoying worm. He was younger than I am, faster on his feet. And I expected a poke in the nose.

"Lord," I said under my breath. "I don't have anything

to say to this man. Give me Your word of wisdom."

The man looked down on me and said, "What do you want?" just like I knew he'd say.

"Doc," I said, "I'd like to come in and talk to you."

"I don't have anything to say to you," he said, and he started to close the door. I stuck my foot in the crack like a rug salesman. I had to get into that man's home. And then the Lord put words in my mouth.

"Doc," I said, "I'm not the kind of person who would be here to ask apologies of you or anyone else, but this is a matter between God and myself, and we'd both appreciate it if you'd let me in." He almost fell over, and I almost fell in.

Those were not my words. That was a word of wisdom direct from heaven, the only words that could have gotten me into that house. We had a good talk, I paid the bill, and confessed to him how I'd been all tangled up with alcohol, in a stupor, and I'd said a lot of unkind things. I wasn't sure just what. But I was there because I had become a Christian—I had met Jesus. I was in a new lifestyle that had to do with getting rid of the muck and garbage of my own making in the past, mending broken relationships and all that. These happened to be two steps in our Alcoholics Anonymous program.

And he said, "Well, I suspected you were having trouble with your drinking, and if we doctors listened to everything that people told us, we'd have to quit or go into an insane asylum." Then he looked straight at me, but not fierce this time, and said, "As far as forgiveness is concerned, it's all forgotten about." Then we shook hands.

When I went out of the doctor's house, I was right with God because I was right with people. My prayer life, my spiritual life, shot up. It had been closed, shut down, until I went and became reconciled.[3]

15

Some Common Obstacles To Living With Joy (Concluded)

Having considered the importance of lack of faith and a guilty conscience as obstacles to living with joy, we turn now to another powerful obstacle.

3. *A Spirit of Unforgiveness.*

This is closely related to a guilty conscience, which grows out of the inability to handle one's own sin, to confess it, ask God's forgiveness, make restitution if possible, and then *forget it!*

The spirit of unforgiveness is a similar inability, this time to handle the sins that other people commit *against us!* For unforgiveness, once having made itself at home in our inner minds and hearts, brings with it a whole train of undesirable spiritual traits and attitudes: irritability, judgmentalism, self-righteousness, vengefulness, resentment, hate, anger.

Resentments and Reactions.

In a devotional book written some thirty years ago, E. Stanley Jones has a helpful section dealing with resentments, and the reactions caused by them. Several excerpts are reprinted below; I have supplied the section titles.

(1) *Effects of Unforgiveness on Health.*

(The author gives a number of startling illustrations of the effects of unforgiveness, resentment, on the good health of those who harbor them. He goes on):

The inner structure of the life is made for good will, not for ill will . . . . When you say, "He makes me sick," that is a fact, for by your reaction of resentment against him the process of digestion is upset and you are sick—literally sick. Again when you say, "He gives me a pain in the neck," that is literally true, for a tension is set up in the neck and pain results. Then again when you say "He certainly is a headache" that is true, for by your reaction to the person concerned your head begins to ache with resentments. On the other hand, when you say, "You're a tonic," it means that you react favorably with appreciation and love and hence the person is a tonic, your whole body is tuned up by good will. Resentments and ill will set you against the structure of universe . . . .

(2) *Self-centeredness: One Cause of Unforgiveness.*

"A tranquil mind is health to the body, but passion is a rot in the bones" (Prov. 15:30). Anger registers itself in the very bones. "A loving mind makes for a healthy body," therefore love is the law of our being. Anger and resentment [unforgiveness] upset the body, and therefore they are not the law of our being.

A lady writes, "I shudder to think what would have happened to me had I not discovered that my self-centeredness and my supersensitivity were undermining my physical and spiritual well-being."

(She had recently had a deep, life-changing religious

experience at one of the "Ashrams" conducted by E. Stanley Jones, which shocked her into realizing that she was "emotionally and spiritually immature." Her story continues):

"I was resentful of the time and attention my husband gave to his profession as a doctor, and not to me. But since I've surrendered all my petty resentments, I'm proud of him and his devotion to his patients. The result is that he and I are really beginning to have a wonderful fellowship." Her resentments had resulted in a facial stroke which left her mouth twisted all out of shape. The face is now normal, for the inside is no longer twisted by resentments.[2]

(3) *Unforgiveness Poisons Life.*

There are those who chew on a resentment for years, and that resentment [unforgiveness] poisons their whole life. A friend tells of being in the home of a wealthy, but crotchety old lady, and as she was about to go to bed, the old lady said: "Would you mind going down to see if the front door is locked, for I can't trust my niece, for she left the front door open once, and burglars might have entered and robbed us." That omission was 38 years before, and the old lady chewed on it for 38 years—and poisoned herself and her surroundings. One moment of quiet talk and forgiveness and the whole thing would have been cleansed away. But the catharsis never came, and the punishment was the thing itself. She lived with an ugly self for 38 years, upsetting herself and everybody around her.[3]

(4) *The Prodigal Son.*

(In commenting on Jesus' parable of the Prodigal Son, E. Stanley Jones points out):

The younger brother in the parable committed wrong actions and the elder brother wrong reactions. He reacted into hardness of heart, unforgiveness, and resentment at the coming home of his brother. When the parable was over, the younger brother was on the inside of the father's house, and the elder brother was on the outside. The Church today is filled with people who, priding themselves that they do not act in lying, stealing, drunkenness, adultery, nevertheless react in resentment, anger, self-justification to what happened to them. They need conversions from wrong reactions [especially unforgiveness] in exactly the same way as others need conversion from wrong actions.[4]

The Conditions of Forgiveness.

William Temple emphasizes an important point in the following paragraph:

> There seems to me to be a very surprising feature in most of the books that I have read and the sermons that I have heard on this subject. Over and over again it is said that our Lord promises forgiveness to those who repent.... There is almost complete agreement that the one condition required on our part is repentance. Of course there is in the Gospels an immense insistence on the need for repentance.... But when He [Jesus] is actually speaking about God's forgiveness of us, it is not 'repentance' that He mentions; it is our own forgiveness of those who have injured us. Only one petition in the Lord's Prayer has any condition attached to it: it is the petition for forgiveness, and the condition attached to it is this. No doubt if by repentance we mean all that the word means in the New Testament, it will include a forgiving spirit; for to repent is to change one's outlook and to regard men and the world as God regards them. But everyone can feel that the emphasis would be quite different if the words were 'Forgive us our trespasses for we do truly repent of them.' This would be like saying, 'I am so sorry, and I won't do it again; do forgive me.' In other words, the plea

for forgiveness would rest on an apology and a promise made to God; and that is not the basis on which our Lord bids us rest our plea. It is to rest on our attitude, not towards God, but toward His other children. He is always ready and eager to forgive, but how can He restore us to the freedom and intimacy of the family life if there are other members of the family toward whom we refuse to be friendly?[5]

Jesus' Teachings about Forgiveness.

Even a casual reading of the Gospels will reveal that William Temple's point is well taken. Consider the verses below:

In Matthew's version of the Lord's Prayer, the petition for forgiveness reads:

> ... and forgive us our sins, just as we have forgiven those who have sinned against us. (Matt. 6:12, TLB)

And immediately following the Amen we find this clear statement:

> Your heavenly Father will forgive you if you forgive those who sin against you; but if *you* refuse to forgive *them, he* will not forgive you. (Matt. 6:14-15, TLB)

Mark has this to say:

> But when you are praying, first forgive anyone you are holding a grudge against, so that your Father in heaven will forgive you your sins too. (Mark 11:25, TLB)

And Luke puts it like this:

> Rebuke your brother if he sins, and forgive him if he is sorry. Even if he wrongs you seven times a day and each time turns again and asks for forgiveness, forgive him. (Luke 17:3-4, TLB)

This teaching is also emphasized in Jesus' story in answer to Peter's query about forgiveness:

> Then Peter approached him with the question, "Master, how many times can my brother wrong me and I must forgive him? Would seven times be enough?"
>
> "No," replied Jesus, "not seven times, but seventy times seven! For the kingdom of Heaven is like a king who decided to settle his accounts with his servants. When he had started calling in his accounts, a man was brought to him who owed him millions of dollars. And when it was plain that he had no means of repaying the debt, his master gave orders for him to be sold as a slave, and his wife and children and all his possessions as well, and the money to be paid over. At this the servant fell on his knees before his master, "Oh, be patient with me!" he cried, "and I will pay you back every penny!" Then his master was moved with pity for him, set him free, and canceled the debt.
>
> "But when this same servant had left his master's presence, he found one of his fellow servants who owed him a few dollars. He grabbed him and seized him by the throat, crying, 'Pay up what you owe me!' At this his fellow servant fell down at his feet and implored him, 'Oh, be patient with me, and I will pay you back!' But he refused and went out and had him put in prison until he should repay the debt.
>
> "When the other fellow servants saw what had happened, they were horrified and went and told their master the whole incident. Then his master called him in.
>
> " 'You wicked servant!' he said. 'Didn't I cancel all that debt when you begged me to do so? Oughtn't you to have taken pity on your fellow servant as I, your master, took pity on you?' And his master in anger handed him over to the jailers till he should repay the whole debt. This is how my Heavenly Father will treat you unless you forgive your brother from your heart." (Matt. 18:21-34, JBP)

And, of course, no list of Jesus' teachings about forgiveness could omit His teaching by example from the Cross:

> Father, forgive these people, ... for they don't know what they are doing. (Luke 23:34, TLB)

A True Story.
The most poignantly appealing true story of overcoming a spirit of unforgiveness that has come to my attention is found in Corrie ten Boom's book *The Hiding Place*. Undoubtedly many of you who are reading this book will recall the incident, but I am including it here because it has such a needed lesson for every would-be follower of Jesus that it must never be forgotten.

After the war was over, Corrie ten Boom found herself drawn into the fulfillment of Betsie's dream of a home in Holland for the healing of survivors of the concentration camps, and eventually of a "camp" in Germany. She was also drawn into a wide ministry in many countries telling Betsie's story, and sharing "the things they had learned together," the message that "joy runs deeper than despair." She goes on:

> The hunger for Betsie's story seemed to increase with time.... But the place where the hunger was greatest was Germany. Germany was a land in ruins, cities of ashes and rubble, but more terrifying still minds and hearts of ashes....
>
> It was at a church service in Munich that I saw him, the former S.S. man who had stood guard at the shower room door in the processing center in Ravensbruck. He was the first of our actual jailers that I had seen, since that time. And suddenly it was all there—the roomful of mocking men, the heaps of clothing, Betsie's pain-blanched face.
>
> He came up to me as the church was emptying, beaming and bowing. "How grateful I am for your

message, Fraulein," he said. "To think that, as you say, He has washed my sins away."

His hand was thrust out to shake mine. And I, who had preached so often . . . the need to forgive, kept my hand at my side.

Even as the angry, vengeful thoughts boiled through me, I saw the sin of them. Jesus Christ had died for this man; was I going to ask for more? Lord Jesus, I prayed, forgive me and help me to forgive him.

I tried to smile, I struggled to raise my hand. I could not; I felt nothing, not the slightest spark of warmth or charity. And so again I breathed a silent prayer. Jesus, I cannot forgive him. Give me your forgiveness.

As I took his hand the most incredible thing happened. From my shoulder, along my arm and through my hand a current seemed to pass from me to him, while into my heart sprang a love for this stranger that almost overwhelmed me.

And so I discovered that it is not on our forgiveness any more than on our goodness that the world's healing hinges, but on His. When He tells us to love our enemies, He gives, along with the command, the love itself.[6]

A Prayer for Forgiveness

Father, forgive me—
   for all my unconscious sinning;
   for all my forgetfulness;
   for all my indifference and blindness
     to my brothers' needs;
   for all my deafness to their calls for help;
   for all my centering my life on myself.

And forgive me, Father—
   for my deliberate disobedience;
   for my refusal to accept Thine offered guidance;
   for my stubborn insistence on my own way;
   for deliberate avoidance of the burdens

Thou wouldst have me carry;
for the words that I speak that minister death
instead of life.

Father, forgive me for all my sins,
both of commission and of omission.

And grant me grace, Father—
to grow in my ability to forgive
those who hurt me,
those who ignore me,
those who criticize me,
or belittle me, or ridicule me,
or lie to me, or gossip untruthfully about me.

Take from my heart
all bitterness and resentment;

Give me Thy strength to forgive—and forget.

Make me know that until I can forgive
those who injure me,
I have no right to claim your
forgiveness of me.

Keep me so filled with Thy Holy Spirit
that there is no room for anything
but love and helpfulness.

In Jesus' name. Amen.

       F.M.T.

16

Living With Joy Through the Experience of "Aloneness"

"Aloneness" is an experience that comes to us in many different forms and at many different times in our lives. It is not limited to those who for various reasons find themselves physically isolated from other people. It is possible to experience loneliness, as many of us have discovered, even in the midst of a crowd! But *aloneness* does not necessarily mean *loneliness*.

A Sense of Self-worth.
A friend of mine in her eighties spent much of her time alone. "Lonely?" she used to reply to inquirers, "Oh, no! I'm very good company for myself!" What a tremendously valuable skill of living—the ability to be "good company for oneself!"

Surely the ability to enjoy oneself in aloneness comes, first of all, from a basically wholesome self-regard, a realization of oneself as a child of God, created and loved by the heavenly Father; and secondly by a continuous awareness of the holy companionship of God himself.

A person characterized by feelings of inferiority, a sense of failure, anxieties and bitterness, would find it impossible to achieve contentment and to resist the feelings of loneliness.

The contented person of whatever age, has usually achieved an optimistic thought trend that finds it easy to follow Paul's excellent advice:

> In conclusion, my brothers, fill your minds with those things that are good and that deserve praise: things that are true, noble, right, pure, lovely and honorable. (Phil. 4:8, GNB)

Such a person finds genuine enjoyment in the slowly passing, uneventful days, consciously appreciates simple pleasures, savors moments of beauty, joyously recalls past pleasures, and faces the future serene and unafraid.

WITHOUT a Sense of Self-worth.

But what about those unfortunate individuals who have a poor opinion of themselves, who are guilt-ridden, full of fear and anxiety, gloomy by nature, resentful of slights, and apt to brood over every small hurt. How can they cope with aloneness?

First of all, they *can* learn to follow Paul's advice, and *choose* what their minds meditate on!

To "Chew the Cud". The dictionary gives among other synonyms for *meditate: ruminate.* And the definition of *ruminate* is "to chew the cud: to chew again what has been chewed slightly and swallowed."

The cow ambles over the meadow biting off mouthful after mouthful of the succulent green grass, and swallowing it into a temporary storehouse just "as is." Later, lying peacefully in the shade of a tree, she regurgitates the grass, mouthful by mouthful, and leisurely "chews the cud," extracting every bit of enjoyment and nourishment before she swallows it again into a second stomach where the process of digestion is completed, and the useless waste is finally discarded from the body.

How similar to the process is our human mental feeding! We too go through each day constantly receiving through our senses unselected impressions: things we see, hear, taste, smell and touch. All these we gather in indiscriminately, unthinkingly, often unconsciously, and store away. Later, we may, or we may not, take time to "chew the cud," recalling and reliving the events of the day, seeking to understand what has happened, and to extract from these events their significance in terms of our purpose in life, and their meaning for our future action. This is meditation.[1]

The Cow—and You.

There are important differences between the cud-chewing of the cow and our meditation. The mind, according to those who have made a study of its processes, never completely discards any experience. The happening may be, and frequently is, pushed down into the subconscious, but it is never completely eliminated! The marvelous instrument which is the human brain, permanently records each impression.

Another difference between us and the aforementioned cow, is that we can choose which of the contents of our mental storehouse we will "chew." And this is a tremendous ability. *We need not* relive over and over again the distressing, upsetting events that happen to us. We need not fill our minds with all the sordid details of the latest crime in the newspapers, or the global tragedies so vividly reported on TV, or the latest gossip in the community. We can choose instead to feed our minds on the nourishing items in the day's supply, the good things that have happened; deeds of kindness and helpfulness, the courageous confrontations, and demonstrations of divine love and forgiveness. And this food that nourishes and sustains the healthy mind also feeds and strengthens the spirit.

We *can* with God's help, cast out of our minds the poisonous thoughts that create and nourish fears, resentments, bitterness, and fill them instead with awareness of the reality of God, of His love for us, and of His ample provision for our every need.[2]

Loneliness-destroying activities.
Once we have determined to control the thoughts of our minds, there are a number of "loneliness-destroying activities" that can help us in our effort to overcome any tendency toward loneliness.

1. *Occupational Therapy.* When I was growing up, no one (I believe) had ever heard of "occupational therapy," but my mother knew all about the danger of Satan's finding "mischief for idle hands to do." And so we girls (three of us) acquired a number of skills for which I have been exceedingly grateful ever since. My mother was an expert needle-woman, and we were introduced at various times to a number of sewing skills—hemstitching, embroidery, smocking—as well as to knitting, crocheting, beadwork, and wood-burning. So we early learned the joy of creative crafts.

Projects of this kind that are tied in with service activities (perhaps in connection with some mission of the local church) have an additional element of enjoyment and are valuable in counteracting any sense of uselessness that may be troubling the older person. I had a dear old auntie who spent the last few years of her long life, knitting sweaters for the Red Cross. Many soldiers and other persons in need were the recipients of her handwork, and were grateful for it.

2. *Using Radio, Television, Tape Recorders.* Modern miracles in communication are available in our generation and can be a blessing to lonely people wherever they are. A tape recorder lends itself to creative use in a number of ways. Tapes are available in many libraries or can be purchased from a number of sources, dealing with every conceivable interest. The whole Bible has been recorded, and countless other books, Shakespeare's plays, volumes of poetry—the list is endless. And the tape recorder has this advantage over both the radio and television: that you can choose what you want to hear, when you want to hear it.

Before her recent death, my older sister, who lived to be ninety, lost her eyesight. She lived with her married daughter and her husband. One Christmas I sent her a tape recorder as my gift, and included in it a tape with my personal Christmas greeting recorded on it.

That was the beginning of a series of recordings by various members of her family that were a source of great joy to her, and shortened the long hours of her final illness. She loved poetry, and one of her grandchildren recorded a number of her favorite poems. A group of her grandchildren recorded their favorite Christmas carols, accompanied by guitars.

It turned out to be a project that gave her joy far beyond our expectations. The letters, recorded on tapes, were almost as good as visits. (The recording proved to be very easy.)

3. *Letter-writing.* One "loneliness-destroying activity" that can prove useful is letter-writing. Most of us look

forward with anticipation to the influx of mail at Christmas time. The family letters and photographs, the brief, scrawled messages, even the cards with just a signature, all combine to spread a network of friendly ties that give us a warm sense of manifold relationships.

Such friendly greetings, however, need not be limited to the Christmas season. Pick out two or three of the loneliest persons you can think of and your effort to relieve their loneliness with occasional friendly letters will ease your own feelings of "aloneness."

Surely, with so many possibilities for happy, worthwhile activities, every older person should be able to find an occupation which will provide a sense of usefulness, and should be able to declare, "Lonely? Oh, no! I'm very good company for myself!"

The Christian Is Never Alone.

The problem of "aloneness" and the often resulting sin of "loneliness" (which is usually self-pity in disguise) have one, and only one, complete solution, and that is the discovery of the tremendous truth that "the Christian is never alone."

François Malaval, a saint who lived in the middle of the seventeenth century wrote:

> There is a time to speak and a time to be silent, says the Sage; a time to laugh, and a time to weep, a time to sow, and a time to reap. There are fixed times for all things, and it would be manifestly out of order to do at one moment what we ought to do at another. But there is no time in which we ought not to love God and think of Him. We ought to think of Him by day and by night, when we are busy and when we are at rest, in company and in solitude, at all times and in every place. The holy companionship of God never wearies us, never embarrasses us; it is not troublesome nor bitter nor inconvenient,

and when we take it with us in our familiar thoughts it has the blessed property of mingling with whatever we are doing; it never separates itself from our affairs, not even from our most trifling conversations.

But in what way, they ask, are we always to think of God, so that this continual application shall not greatly interfere with our worldly life? Think of Him often, and such thoughts will not disturb or deflect you; they will rather accompany you, go before you, follow you, and generally awaken you. If someone ordered you to make twenty-five or thirty respirations every minute, you would repulse such a suggestion; you would think it would impede all your actions. Yet you breathe every moment without noticing it, and you do not cease to act with as much liberty as if nothing were going on in you.[3]

So it is with the Christian's continuous awareness of the holy companionship of God.

Poustinia.
"Being good company for myself" is a partial and superficial answer to anyone's problem of loneliness but it leaves the main cause of the problem untouched. For loneliness is usually part of a greater sin, the sin of self-centeredness, seeing everything that happens only in its relationship to ourselves. The only permanent cure lies in dethroning Self, and in making God the center of our lives, in developing in oneself the continuous awareness of "the holy companionship of God."

All the saints down through the ages have been aware of God's steady, never-failing, always available companionship, and much helpful advice has been written on how to nurture a continual sense of His presence. The Bible, in a brief eight words, sums up an important directive found in many writings:

Be still, and know that I am God . . . . (Ps. 46:10, KJV)

My own vivid realization of both the importance and the joyousness of this awareness of God was deepened recently when I read a book, *Poustinia* written by a modern "saint," a Russian Catholic, Catherine de Hueck Doherty. The word *Poustinia* is Russian, meaning literally *desert*, but also having a much deeper meaning: "a quiet, holy place that people wish to enter to find the God who dwells within them."

Catherine Doherty writes:

> In the last few years, I have been talking and writing a great deal about silence, solitude, and deserts . . . because I think they are vitally important to our growing, changing, technological urban civilization. (Page 18)
>
> It seems strange to say, but what can help modern man find the answers to his own mystery and the mystery of him in whose image he is created, is *silence, solitude, and desert* . . . .
>
> True silence is the search of man for God.
>
> True silence is a suspension bridge that a soul in love with God builds to cross the dark, frightening gullies of its own mind, the strange chasms of temptation, the depthless precipices of its own fears that impede its way to God . . . .
>
> True silence is a key to the immense and flaming heart of God . . . .
>
> Yes, such silence is holy, a prayer beyond all prayers, leading to the final prayer of constant presence of God, to the heights of contemplation, when the soul, finally at peace, lives by the will of him whom she loves totally, utterly and completely . . . .
>
> Deserts, silence, and solitudes are not necessarily *places, but states of mind and heart*. These deserts can be found in the midst of the city and in every day of our lives. We need only to look for them and realize our tremendous

need for them. They will be small solitudes, little deserts, tiny pools of silence, but the experience they will bring if we are disposed to enter them, may be as exultant and as holy as all the deserts of the world, even the one God Himself entered. For it is God who makes solitude, deserts, and silences holy . . . .

Silence is sometimes the absence of speech—but it is always the act of listening. The mere absence of noise (which is empty of listening to the voice of God) is not silence . . . .

Deserts, solitude, silence. For a soul that realizes the tremendous need of all three, opportunities present themselves in the midst of the congested trappings of all the world's immense cities.

But how, really, can one achieve such solitude? *By standing still!*

Stand still and allow the strange, deadly restlessness of our tragic age to fall away like the worn out, dusty cloak that it is . . . .

Stand still, and look deep into the motivations of life. Are they such that true foundations of sanctity can be built on them? For truly man has been born to be a saint—a lover of Love, who died for us! There is but one tragedy—not to be a saint! . . .

Stand still, and lifting your hands and heart to God, pray that the mighty wind of the Holy Spirit may clear all the cobwebs of fears, selfishness, greed, narrowheartedness, away from the soul; that his tongues of flame may descend to give courage to begin again.

All this standing still can be done in the midst of the outward noise of daily living, and the duties of state in life. For it will bring order into the soul, God's order, and God's order will bring tranquility, his own tranquility.[4]

Aloneness in Old Age.

The experience of aloneness is by no means limited to the elderly; many a teen-ager knows full well the bitterness of feeling ignored and rejected. It is nevertheless true that those to whom is given the "gift of long life" also experience in addition to the narrowing circles of activity, the gradual loss through death of many beloved friends.

Everything that has been said about aloneness, applies especially to the growing numbers of people, sixty, seventy, eighty and ninety+ who are euphemistically referred to as "senior citizens," (of whom I am one. My 91st birthday is rapidly approaching!)

Recently I came across an anonymous "Prayer for Old Age" which seemed to express my feelings so precisely that I am including it here, hoping that it may prove useful to many old and not-so-old people.

Prayer for Old Age

O God, my heavenly Father, whose gift is length of days, help me to make the noblest use of mind and body in my advancing years.

According to my strength apportion Thou my work.

As Thou hast pardoned my transgressions, sift the ingatherings of my memory that evil may grow dim and good may shine forth clearly.

I bless Thee for Thy gifts and especially for Thy presence; and the love of friends in heaven and earth. Grant me new ties of friendship, new opportunities of service, joy in the growth and happiness of children, sympathy with those who bear the burdens of the world, clear thought, and quiet faith.

Teach me to bear infirmities with cheerful patience.

Keep me from narrow pride in outgrown ways; blind eyes that will not see the good of change; impatient judgments of the methods of others.

Let Thy peace rule my spirit through all the days of my waning powers.

Take from me all fear of death, and all despair or undue love of life; that with a glad heart at rest in Thee, I may await Thy will concerning me. Through Jesus Christ my Lord. Amen.[5]

In Conclusion.

Rejoice—in *aloneness?* Only if we sturdily reject every temptation to feel loneliness, realizing that *the Christian is never alone!* Only if we welcome every interval of silence and solitude as a pure blessing (instead of deeming it an affliction!), and thank God for it as an opportunity to practice the consciousness of His loving, continuous presence with us.

Jesus knew aloneness. He also knew the holy companionship of God. In His last talk with His disciples on the night of His betrayal, He said:

Behold, the hour cometh, yea, is now come, that ye shall be scattered, every man to his own, and shall leave me alone; and yet *I am not alone, because the Father is with me.* (John 16:32, KJV; italics added)

17

Living With Joy Through the Experience of Bereavement

At no time in your life is your witness for Christ more important than when death takes someone you love. That is the supreme test of the depth and reality of your faith. If we "believe our beliefs," excessive grief cannot have dominion over us. Praising God for all things, secure in His love and His promise of eternal life, we can victoriously refuse to grieve like those with no hope.

The Glory of Easter.

We may search our New Testaments in vain for any of the gloomy graveyard images, the shadows, the darkness, the pains, the bitterness of death, which still appear in many of our Christian hymns. There is no death for the Christian: it has ... been completely abolished ....

The glory of Easter is not a pious hope that we shall somehow survive after a fear-ridden journey through the "gloomy portal." It is a demonstration of undiluted joy. Christ is the one who bore the sin, the darkness, the terror, and the pain. He is the one who "tasted death for every man."

Must we always dim and tarnish the glory of God's magnificent promises with our mental reservations and our secret fears?

What stops us from accepting the simple fact "Jesus Christ hath abolished death"?

Rejoice in the glory of Easter![1]

To Die Is Gain.

Death is no respecter of persons when he comes knocking at the door. Death comes to all. If we have the right perspective of death, a channel of clear thinking about it, and a right relationship with God, we are going to view death as a passageway to glory . . . .

Death is like a ship that leaves port bound for a world cruise. Friends come to the dock to wish the traveler "Bon voyage." They cry, they weep, they wave handkerchiefs back and forth . . . . The ship begins to leave port. When one dies the ship of the soul goes away. We mourn for the loved one. Yet there are others on the other side of the sea, who are waving their handkerchiefs beckoning the ship to come in with its passengers. We mourn here because our loved ones pass into the distance beyond our sight. On the other shore are people who say, "Come on, come on; we have been waiting for you!"

When we die we go into the presence of God . . . . We see God . . . . It is not death to die . . . . To die is gain. Amen.[2]

How to Get Through Your Struggles.

In the first chapter of this book, Oral Roberts tells "How in the worst struggle Evelyn and I ever had, we discovered Jesus walking on the water, and learned that we could walk on the water, too" (see Matt. 14:25). In this chapter there is a deeply moving account of his and his wife's response to the news, brought early one morning by the police, that their daughter and son-in-law had been killed when a plane in which they had been traveling exploded. Their deaths left parentless three children aged thirteen, eight and five. The account of how the couple faced this tragedy is too long to be included here, but there follows a summary by the author of some of what they learned through the experience:

Putting It All Together for Myself

I can learn to "walk on the water" as Jesus did.

* * *

I can face the night and the storm, knowing that sunsets only make for more sunrises.

* * *

I have hope—the blessed hope of the Resurrection.

* * *

I can go to God for help and hope because I know He is greater than any problem or need I have. He will see me through any storm I face.

* * *

I can say, "God knows something about this that I don't know."

* * *

I can look the world in the eye and say, "God will come to me walking on the water, He is always there when I need Him the most . . . ."[3]

Heaven.

Heaven is not fitly symbolized by a *place* to which men travel separately. Heaven is the universal fellowship of all spirits in the Love of the Divine Spirit . . . . The individual who has really and fully surrendered his heart to God has not only attained the goal of his destiny so far as circumstances permit, but finding in God the assurance of the end and the eternal perfection, he also finds for himself the fruition of perfect joy and peace . . . .

Christ's Resurrection has proved that human nature, when indwelt by God, conquers death. Our hope of immortality rests on this revelation of what is possible, and on the love of God to make it actual. For if God loves, He will not let the object of His love be abolished out of existence . . . .

If, therefore, a man has learnt the true goal of his being and is seeking to open his heart to God so that God may dwell in him and he in God, he knows that he has all Time before him in which to explore the riches of the Divine Love which to all ages he never will exhaust. He has the everlasting years before him, and he has God with him all the way.[4]

The Everlasting Arms.

The eternal God is thy refuge, and underneath are the everlasting arms . . . . (Deut. 33:27, KJV)

This Bible verse has become clear to me because it is always associated in my mind with two very precious memories—one of my very early childhood, and the other in my early eighties.

It was late in the evening—long past my usual early bedtime. The family (my mother, my father, my two older sisters and I) were returning home. From where? I am not sure. Perhaps from a family gathering at Grandma Flandreau's home in a nearby city.

I was—how old? Not more than three, I believe. It is a flash memory, very brief—a feeling memory mostly, hardly more than a momentary re-creation of the situation. I remember the darkness, relieved only by the occasional dim flicker of inadequate street lights. I was aware of the stillness, and of occasional unfamiliar night sounds.

I knew dimly that "mama" and the girls were there, walking beside us. But mostly I was aware only of an all-pervasive sense of well-being, of complete and happy relaxation, for my small self was being carried by my father, firmly held in his strong arms, snuggled contentedly against his shoulder, in a dim, half-asleep, half-awake consciousness, completely happy. A flash memory, distinct and vivid, miraculously preserved for more than eighty years!

And the feeling tone of that memory was duplicated in vivid reality the night (several years ago now) when my husband died.

Two years or so previously I had had a startling realization that the inexorable process of deterioration had speeded up and that the superb strength of George's physical body was draining away. In the weeks and months that followed, as he grew rapidly more feeble, I found myself praying earnestly and repeatedly the same prayer: "Father, don't let anything happen to me! Don't take me home first! Let me live to take care of George to the end of his life!"

The months passed, and the night came when my daughter Bette and I stood beside George's bed, knowing that the end was imminent. We listened to his difficult breathing. It stopped—and we held our breath. But then it started again—three or four more long struggling breaths—and then silence—deep, permanent silence. And my heart almost stopped too.

And it was at that precise moment that awareness of God's immediate presence and love flooded my heart, and a totally unexpected, and almost unbelievable, peace welled up inside me, and God's voice spoke unmistakably in my innermost being: "This is my answer to your prayer." And through my tears I answered in all sincerity, "Thank you, Father."

And in that moment I knew, with an intensity I never could have imagined possible, the reality of the everlasting arms of my heavenly Father, enfolding me in His love. And I wept with a strange mixture of intense grief and upwelling gratitude—accepting the reality of George's death because of a second reality of God's comforting and sustaining presence.

Two memories, one near the beginning of my life, and one near its end, more than eighty years later. Separate memories, but not unrelated. How I praise God for my relationship to human parents whose dependable love drew from me responsive love and trust, and made possible my later faith in the Father-God!

Biblical Comfort for Times of Bereavement.

> There is none like unto . . . God . . . .
> The eternal God is thy refuge, and underneath are the everlasting arms . . . . (Deut. 33:26-27, KJV)
>
> Precious in the sight of the Lord is the death of his saints . . . . Praise ye the Lord. (Ps. 116:15, 19, KJV)

Jesus said:

> Let not your heart be troubled: ye believe in God, believe also in me.
> In my Father's house are many mansions: if it were not so, I would have told you. I go to prepare a place for you.
> And if I go and prepare a place for you, I will come again, and receive you unto myself; that where I am, there ye may be also . . . .
> Peace I leave with you, my peace I give unto you: not as the world giveth, give I unto you. Let not your heart be troubled, neither let it be afraid. (John 14:1-3, 27, KJV)
>
> Now this I say, brethren, that flesh and blood cannot inherit the kingdom of God; neither doth corruption

inherit incorruption.

For this corruptible must put on incorruption, and this mortal must put on immortality.

So when this corruptible shall have put on incorruption, and this mortal shall have put on immortality, then shall be brought to pass the saying that is written, Death is swallowed up in victory.

O death, where is thy sting? O grave, where is thy victory?

... Thanks be to God, which giveth us the victory through our Lord Jesus Christ. (1 Cor. 15:50, 53-55, 57, KJV)

And I saw a new heaven and a new earth: for the first heaven and the first earth were passed away; and there was no more sea.

And I John saw the holy city, new Jerusalem, coming down from God out of heaven, prepared as a bride adorned for her husband.

And I heard a great voice out of heaven, saying, Behold, the tabernacle of God is with men, and he will dwell with them, and they shall be his people, and God himself shall be with them, and be their God.

And God shall wipe away all tears from their eyes; and there shall be no more death, neither sorrow, nor crying, neither shall there be any more pain: for the former things are passed away.

And he that sat upon the throne said, Behold, I make all things new. (Rev. 21:1-5, KJV)

A Prayer of Thanksgiving.

Thank you, Father,
> For the blessed assurance that to be "absent from the body" is to be "present with the Lord";
> For the sure knowledge that "flesh and blood cannot inherit the kingdom of God" but that "this corruptible must put on incorruption, and this mortal must put on immortality";

For the triumphant understanding that "Death is swallowed up in victory";
For the shining promise of eternal life when you will "wipe away all tears from our eyes; and there shall be no more death, neither sorrow nor crying, neither any more pain" for you will "make all things new."
Praise your holy name, Lord! Amen.

Part IV

"*Our Father*": *Prayers of Faith and Joy*

18

"Lord, Teach Us to Pray"

> And it came to pass, that, as he was praying in a certain place, when he ceased, one of his disciples said unto him, Lord, teach us to pray . . . . (Luke 11:1, KJV)

"Teach us to pray." What an odd request from those Jewish disciples! For of course they had been taught to pray almost from babyhood. Every Jewish child grew up in a home where prayer was woven into the fabric of daily life. There were traditional prayers for use before meals, when washing the hands, when going in and out of the house, and countless others. So what did the disciples mean when they demanded, "Lord, teach us to pray"? They were asking, "Lord, teach us to pray *as you do*, in a way that channels to us and through us, the Divine Power."[1]

It was at this time that Jesus gave the disciples the Lord's Prayer. In the Matthew version it is made up of just sixty-six words. Notice that nine of these are "our," "us," and "we"; there is not a single "I," "we," or "mine" in it. This is not a prayer of personal, selfish petition. If we pray it rightly it is a prayer for ourselves, and for all of God's people throughout the world.

The Lord's Prayer

Our Father, which art in heaven, Hallowed be thy name.

Thy kingdom come. Thy will be done in earth, as it is in heaven.

Give us this day our daily bread.

And forgive us our debts, as we forgive our debtors.

And lead us not into temptation, but deliver us from evil: For thine is the kingdom, and the power, and the glory for ever. Amen. (Matt. 6:9-13, KJV)

Morgan Phelps Noyes, in a series of sermons on the Lord's Prayer, once wrote:

> The one thing his disciples asked Jesus to teach them was the art of prayer. They came to him saying, "Lord, teach us to pray." He gave them a form of words which we call the Lord's Prayer . . . .
>
> There is always a danger in using forms of words in prayer. We become so familiar with them that we rattle them off without stopping to remember what they mean. This is what has happened to the Lord's Prayer. Words can be nothing but meaningless sounds. But they can also be ladders for the spirit. So Jesus gave his disciples a model prayer, and taught them that when they put themselves into his words, his words could become their prayer, linking them in spirit with the living God.

This section consists of a number of prayers of faith and joy, for the enrichment of your personal prayer life. These too are "forms of words." It is possible to repeat them, and have them meaningless words. Only as you are aware that you are speaking to the ever-present living God do they become prayer. "Lord, teach us to pray."

"Our Father": Prayers of Faith and Joy.

The prayers in the following pages are gathered into

four sections:
1. Biblical Prayers.
2. Prayers of the Saints.
3. Prayers from Various Sources.
4. Prayer Hymns.

A number of the prayers have been slightly altered—usually from plural to singular—in order to make them more strongly personal. Titles of the prayers have been supplied by the compiler.

1
Biblical Prayers

Thou hast put gladness in my heart.... (Ps. 4:7a, KJV)

I will praise thee, O LORD, with my whole heart; I will shew forth all thy marvellous works.

I will be glad and rejoice in thee: I will sing praise to thy name, O thou most High. (Ps. 9:1-2, KJV)

... Make everyone rejoice who puts his trust in you. Keep them shouting for joy because you are defending them. Fill all who love you with your happiness. For you bless the godly man, O Lord; you protect him with your shield of love. (Ps. 5:11, TLB)

Thou hast turned for me my mourning into dancing: thou hast put off my sackcloth, and girded me with gladness.

To the end that my glory may sing praise to thee, and not be silent. O LORD my God, I will give thanks unto thee for ever. (Ps. 30:11-12, KJV)

Be gracious to me, O God, according to Thy lovingkindness;
According to the greatness of Thy compassion blot out my transgressions.
Wash me thoroughly from my iniquity,
And cleanse me from my sin ...
Against Thee, Thee only, I have sinned,

And done what was evil in Thy sight . . .
Wash me, and I shall be whiter than snow.
Make me to hear joy and gladness . . .
Restore to me the joy of Thy salvation. (Ps. 51, NAS—selected verses)

Lord, I trust in you alone . . . . I worship only you . . . . I am radiant with joy because of your mercy, for you have listened to my troubles and have seen the crisis in my soul.

Oh, how great is your goodness . . . . For you have stored up great blessings for those who trust and reverence you. (Ps. 31:1, 6-7, 19, TLB)

O satisfy me early with Thy mercy; that I may rejoice and be glad all my days.

Make me glad according to the days wherein thou hast afflicted me, and the years wherein I have seen evil. (Ps. 90:14-15—altered, KJV)

Your steadfast love, O Lord, is as great as all the heavens. Your faithfulness reaches beyond the clouds. . . . Your decisions are as full of wisdom as the oceans are with water . . . . How precious is your constant love, O God! All humanity takes refuge in the shadow of your wings. You feed them with blessings from your own table and let them drink from your rivers of delight. (Ps. 36:5-9, TLB)

God, be merciful to us, and bless us; and cause thy face to shine upon us;

That thy way may be known upon earth, thy saving health among all nations.

Let the people praise thee, O God; let all the people praise thee.

O let the nations be glad and sing for joy: for thou shalt judge the people righteously, and govern the nations upon earth.

Let the people praise thee, O God; let all the people praise thee . . . . (Ps. 67—altered, KJV)

Be gracious to me, O Lord,
For to Thee I cry all day long.
Make glad the soul of Thy servant,
For to Thee, O Lord, I lift up my soul.
For Thou, O Lord, art good, and ready to forgive,
And abundant in lovingkindness to all who call
   upon Thee. (Ps. 86:3-5, NAS)

I cling to your commands and follow them as closely as I can. Lord, don't let me make a mess of things . . . .

Just tell me what to do and I will do it, Lord. As long as I live I'll wholeheartedly obey. Make me walk along the right paths for I know how delightful they really are . . . .

Your laws are my joyous treasure for ever. (Ps. 119:31-35, 111, TLB)

Father, I pray that I may be filled with the knowledge of thy will, and all wisdom and spiritual understanding;

That I may walk worthy of my Lord unto all pleasing, being fruitful in every good work, and increasing in the knowledge of thee;

Strengthened with all might according to thy glorious power, unto all patience and longsuffering with joyfulness;

Giving thanks unto thee, who hast made me meet to be a partaker of the inheritance of the saints in light:

Who hath delivered me from the power of darkness, and hath translated me into the kingdom of thy dear Son . . . . Amen. (See Col. 1:9-13, KJV—Altered.)

2
Prayers of the Saints

Note: All the prayers in this section are reprinted from the series of small booklets: *Great Devotional Classics* (Nashville, Tenn.: The Upper Room).

O thou everlasting Light, Surpassing all created lights, dart the beams of thy brightness from above, to pierce all the most inward parts of my heart. Purify, rejoice, enlighten my spirit with all the powers thereof, that I may cleave unto thee with abundance of joy and triumph.[2]

Eternal God of Life, may I die daily to my selfish, fearful, despairing self and become resurrected to my Christian self filled with love, peace, joy, power.[3]

Eternal and most merciful God, I hear thy voice calling me to be a saint. May I possess the radiance, courage, compassion, unselfishness, self-discipline, humility, and devotion characteristic of the saints. As they found heaven on earth, so may I . . . . Amen.[4]

Eternal God, in whom Jesus Christ kept his faith, even in the dark moments on the Cross, help me to have faith like his . . . . Help me to remember that when the night is darkest, thy stars in the heavens shine most brilliantly. . . . Amen.[5]

Good God! What a mighty felicity this is to which we are called! How graciously hast thou joined our duty and happiness together, and prescribed that for our work the performance whereof is a great reward! . . . Oh, the happiness of those souls that have broken the fetters of self-love and disentangled their affection from every narrow and particular good! Whose understandings are enlightened by the Holy Spirit, and their wills enlarged to the extent of thine! Who love thee above all things, and all mankind for thy sake! . . . O teach me to do thy will, for thou art my God . . . . Lead me into the land of brightness . . . . Amen.[6]

A Pilgrimage of Love

O Christ, Thou art the Joy of every longing heart. Thou art ever with me, and as I am receptive and obedient to Thee, my days here become a pilgrimage of love and service in preparation for the life to come. I thank Thee for this joyous and meaningful communion with Thee.

Thou art indeed the Lord of my life, and the shepherd of my soul. Amen.[7]

Renew My Mind and Heart

O Lord, my God, in whom I find my peace and joy; this is the day which Thou hast made; I will be glad and rejoice in it. Save me from every unkind temper and from every dismal thought. Renew my mind and heart that I may live in both happiness and holiness. I thank Thee for Thy great mercy and for the continuous rejoicing that is mine in Thy dear Son Jesus Christ my Saviour. Amen.[8]

3
Prayers From Various Sources

At the Rising of the Sun

O Lord Jesus, Creator of all things, highest of the glory of the Father in heaven: I thank Thee with my whole heart that Thou permittest me again to see the joyous sunlight. O bright Son of Righteousness, arise and shine in my heart, also, that, in Thy refulgence, I may walk as a child of light as in the day, and finally behold Thee blessed in the eternal light of joy everlasting. Amen.[9]

For the Joy of Our Lord

Help us this day, O God, to serve Thee devoutly, and the world busily. May we do our work wisely, give succour secretly, go to meat appetitely, sit thereat discretely, arise temperately, please our friend duly, go to bed merrily, and sleep surely; for the joy of the Lord, Jesus Christ. Amen.[10]

A Perpetual Contentedness

O God, animate me to cheerfulness. May I have a joyful sense of my own blessings, learn to look on the bright circumstances of my lot, and maintain a perpetual contentedness under Thy allotments. Fortify my mind against disappointments and calamity. Preserve me from despondency, from yielding to dejection. Teach me that no evil is intolerable but a guilty conscience; and that nothing can hurt me if, with true loyalty of affection, I keep Thy commandments and take refuge in Thee. Amen.[11]

For a Sense of Joy

Grant to me, O Lord, the royalty of inward happiness, and the serenity which comes from living close to thee. Daily renew in me the sense of joy, and let the eternal spirit of the Father dwell in my soul and body, filling me with light and grace, so that, bearing about with me the infection of a good courage, I may be a diffuser of life, and may meet all ills and cross accidents with gallant and high-hearted happiness, giving thee thanks always for all things. Amen.[12]

For Courage

Make me ready for the great adventure of living . . . . Among the immediate and incidental problems of personal living, give me courage to face the facts which confront me without evasions or self-deception . . . Among the perplexities of daily life give me equanimity and self-control, that I may not be a slave of circumstances but their master, with the exhilaration of conflict and the joy of victory . . . . Amen.[13]

From Joy to Joy

Creative Spirit, who are ever at work in Thy world, fashioning out of ion and electron forms of wonder and of beauty, Thou who can bring light out of darkness, joy out of sorrow, righteousness out of sin, I thank Thee for Thy gift of life. Thou, to whose power there are no limits, make of me this day what Thou wouldst have me to be.

Forgetting the things that are behind, may I press on to the things that are before, and renewing my spirit through contact with Thy divine Spirit, go from strength to strength and from joy to joy. Amen.[14]

Delightful unto Thee

O Adorable and Eternal God! Hast Thou made me a free agent? . . . To make a world for me was much . . . to prepare eternal joys for me was more. But to give me a power to displease Thee . . . is more stupendous than all these . . . . Hereby Thou hast prepared a new fountain and torrent of joys greater than all that went before . . . . O Thou who art infinitely delightful to the sons of men, make me, and the sons of men, infinitely delightful unto Thee . . . . Amen.[15]

True Happiness

O send Thy light and Thy truth, that I may live always near to Thee, my God . . . . Lord, let me have no will of my own; or consider my true happiness as depending on the smallest degree on anything that can befall me outwardly, but in consisting altogether in conforming to Thy will. Amen.[16]

The Thornbush Aflame

O God, I thank thee for this universe, our great home: for its vastness, and its riches, and for the manifoldness of the life which teems upon it and of which I am a part. I praise thee for the arching sky and the blessed winds, for the driving clouds and the constellations on high . . . . I thank thee for my senses by which I can see the splendour of the morning, and hear the jubilant songs of love, and smell the breath of the springtime. Grant me, I pray thee, a heart wide open to all this joy and beauty, and save my soul from being so steeped in care or so darkened by passion, that I pass heedless and unseeing when even the thornbush by the wayside is aflame with thy glory. Amen.[17]

For Cheerfulness

O God, renew my spirit by Thy Holy Spirit, and draw my heart this morning unto Thyself, that my work may not be a burden, but a delight; and give me such a mighty love to Thee as may sweeten all my obedience. Let me not serve with the spirit of bondage as a slave, but with cheerfulness and gladness as a child delighting myself in Thee and rejoicing in Thy wishes for the sake of Jesus Christ.[18]

For the Joy of Living

O Thou Creator of all things that are, I lift my heart in gratitude to Thee for this day's happiness:
  For the mere joy of living;
  For all the sights and sounds around me;
  For friendship and good company;
  For work to perform, and the skill and strength to perform it;
  For a time to play when the day's work was done, and for strength and a glad heart to enjoy it.
  Yet let me never think, O eternal Father, that I am here to stay. Let me still remember that I am a stranger and pilgrim on the earth. For here we have no continuing city, but we seek one to come. Preserve me by Thy grace, good Lord, from so losing myself in the joys of the earth that I may have no longing left for the finer joys of heaven. Let not the happiness of this day become a snare to my worldly heart . . . .
  I thank Thee, O Lord . . . for the sure promise of an endless life which Thou hast given me in the glorious gospel of Jesus Christ my Lord. Amen.[19]

On My Way Rejoicing

O God the Father, who alone satisfieth the desires of every living thing, who ordainest my strength for Thy service and grantest me intervals of rest for the renewal of my strength; Sanctify, I beseech Thee, to Thy glory my labor and my rest, my seriousness and my mirth, my sorrow and my joy, and send me forth with Thy blessing, that I may go on my way rejoicing. Amen.[20]

The Spirit of Joy

O God . . . help me to keep my heart clean, and to live so honestly and fearlessly that no outward failure can dishearten me, or take away the joy of conscious integrity. Open wide the eyes of my soul that I may see good in all things. Grant me this day some new vision of Thy truth; inspire me with the spirit of joy and gladness. Amen.[21]

It Is Thee I Crave

O Thou divine Spirit, that in all events of life art knocking at the door of my heart, help me to respond to Thee. I would not be driven blindly as the stars over their courses. I would not be made to work out Thy will unwillingly, to fulfill Thy law unintelligently, to obey mandates unsympathetically. I would take the events of my life as good and perfect gifts from Thee; I would receive even the sorrows of life as disguised gifts from Thee. I would have my heart open at all times to receive—at morning, noon and night; in spring and summer and winter. Whether Thou comest to me in sunshine or in rain, I would take Thee into my heart joyfully. Thou art Thyself more than the sunshine, Thou art Thyself compensation for the rain. It is Thee and not Thy gifts I crave; knock and I shall open unto Thee. Amen.[22]

All My Heart's Desire

In Thy will, O Lord, is my peace.
In Thy love is my rest.
In Thy service is my joy.
Thou art all my heart's desire... Amen.[23]

The Hebrew Morning Service

Though our mouths were full of song as the sea, and our tongues of exultation as the multitude of its waves, and our lips of praise as the wide-extended firmament; though our eyes shone with light like the sun and the moon, and our hands were spread forth like the eagles of heaven, and our feet were swift as winds, we should still be unable to thank Thee and to bless Thy name, O Lord our God and God of our fathers, for one-thousandth or one ten-thousandth part of the bounties which Thou hast bestowed upon our fathers and upon us.[24]

Joy Amid Trials

O Lord, Jesus Christ, with my whole heart I pray Thee, evermore speak this joy of heaven unto my heart, and write it in golden letters of faith, upon my soul, that, as a child of God and heir to eternal life, I may, in the midst of trials, always have Thy joyful comfort in my heart, and a peaceful conscience in my body, to the end that I may overcome all temptation and adversity with joyful patience... and at last in Thine own good time, end my days in gladsome hope. Amen.[25]

4
Prayer Hymns

Fill Me, Radiancy Divine

Christ, whose glory fills the skies,
   Christ, the true, the only light,
Sun of Righteousness, arise,
   Triumph o'er the shades of night;
Day-spring from on high, be near,
Day-star, in my heart appear.

Dark and cheerless is the morn
   Unaccompanied by Thee;
Joyless is the day's return,
   Till Thy mercy's beams I see;
Till Thou inward light impart,
Glad my eyes, and warm my heart.

Visit then this soul of mine,
   Pierce the gloom of sin and grief;
Fill me, Radiancy Divine,
   Scatter all my unbelief;
More and more Thyself display,
Shining to the perfect day.[26]

O Master Workman of the Race

O Master Workman of the race,
   Thou Man of Galilee,
Who, with the eyes of early youth,
   Eternal things didst see;
We thank Thee for Thy boyhood faith
   That shone Thy whole life through:
"Did ye not know it is My work
   My Father's work to do?"

O Carpenter of Nazareth,
   Builder of life divine,
Who shapest man to God's own law,
   Thyself the fair design,
Build us a tower of Christlike height,
   That we the land may view,
And see, like Thee, our noblest work,
   Our Father's work to do.

O Thou who dost the vision send,
   And givest each his task,
And with the task sufficient strength:
   Show us Thy will, we ask;
Give us a conscience bold and good;
   Give us a purpose true,
That it may be our highest joy
   Our Father's work to do. Amen.[27]

Jesus, Thou Joy of Loving Hearts

Jesus, Thou Joy of loving hearts!
   Thou fount of life! Thou light of men!
From the best bliss that earth imparts
   We turn, unfilled, to Thee again.

O Jesus, ever with us stay;
   Make all our moments calm and bright;
Chase the dark night of sin away,
   Shed o'er the world Thy holy light!

Jesus, our only joy be Thou,
   As Thou our prize wilt be;
Jesus, be Thou our glory now,
   And through eternity.[28]

Joyful, Joyful, We Adore Thee

God of Glory, God of love;
Hearts unfold like flowers before Thee,
  Opening to the sun above.
Melt the clouds of sin and sadness;
  Drive the dark of doubt away;
Giver of immortal gladness,
  Fill us with the light of day.
All Thy works with joy surround Thee,
  Earth and heaven reflect Thy rays.
Stars and angels sing around Thee,
  Center of unbroken praise.
Field and forest, vale and mountain,
  Flowery meadow, flashing sea,
Chanting bird and flowing fountain
  Call us to rejoice in Thee.

Thou art giving and forgiving
  Ever blessing, ever blest,
Well-spring of the joy of living,
  Ocean depth of happy rest!
Thou our Father, Christ our Brother.
  All who live in love are Thine:
Teach us how to love each other,
  Lift us to the joy divine.[29]

O Master, Let Me Walk with Thee

O Master, let me walk with Thee
In lowly paths of service free;
Tell me Thy secret, help me bear
The strain of toil, the fret of care.

Help me the slow of heart to move
By some clear, winning word of love;
Teach me the wayward feet to stay,
And guide them in the homeward way.

Teach me Thy patience; still with Thee
In closer, dearer company,
In work that keeps faith sweet and strong,
In trust that triumphs over wrong;

In hope that sends a shining ray
Far down the future's broadening way;
In peace that only Thou canst give,
With Thee, O Master, let me live. Amen.[30]

Appendix A
A Special Word for Parents

A Special Word for Parents

No heritage you can pass on to your children can compare for a moment with *the ability to live joyously*. As you yourselves grow in your own ability to fulfill the necessary conditions so that joy will flood your own souls, you will at the same time be acquiring the most important characteristic of an effective parent, for such joy is blessedly contagious.

It has long been recognized that:

> The first duty to children is to make them happy. If you have not made them so, you have wronged them. No other good they may get can make up for that.[1]

Joyous Parents.

Erich Fromm has written persuasively of the need for parents who are themselves joyous people:

> Motherly love ... is unconditional affirmation of the child's life and his needs. But one addition to this description must be made here: Affirmation of the child's life has two aspects, one is the care and responsibility absolutely necessary for the preservation of the child's life and his growth. The other aspect goes further than mere preservation. It is the attitude which instills in the child a love of living, which gives him the feeling: it is good to be alive, it is good to be a little boy or girl, it is good to be on this earth! These two aspects of motherly love are expressed very succinctly in the Biblical story of creation. God created the world, and man. This corresponds to the simple care and affirmation of existence. But God goes beyond this minimum requirement. On each day after nature—and man—is created, God says, "It is good." ... Love in this second step makes the child feel: it is good to have been born: it instills in the child the love for life, and not only the wish to remain alive. The same idea may be taken to be expressed in another Biblical symbolism.

The promised land (land is always a mother symbol) is described as "flowing with milk and honey." Milk is the symbol of the first aspect of love, that of care and affirmation. Honey symbolizes the sweetness of life, the love for it, and the happiness of being alive. Most mothers are capable of giving "milk"; but only a minority of giving "honey" too. In order to be able to give honey, a mother must not only be a "good mother" but a happy person—and this aim is not achieved by many. The effect on a child can hardly be exaggerated. Mother's love for life is as infectious as her anxiety is. Both attitudes have a deep effect on the child's whole personality: one can distinguish indeed among children—and adults—those who got only "milk" and those who got "milk and honey."[2]

True joyousness comes from a religious understanding of life which discerns, even though dimly, purpose and meaning beneath all the contradictions and seemingly irrational elements. For centuries the Christian faith has proved for countless thousands the basis of such a joyous orientation of life. This faith is characterized not by a blind and hopeless endurance of evil and suffering, but by an illumined recognition that life is primarily a school, in which even the grimmest lessons can be productive of spiritual growth and moral power.

Surely no other legacy you can leave your children can compare in importance with the legacy of a firm and joyous faith in God and in His beneficent and eternal purposes for His children.

Bible Directives for Parents.
The Bible directives for parents are clear and unmistakable.

> O Israel, listen: Jehovah is our God, Jehovah alone. You must love him with *all* your heart, soul and might. And

you must think constantly about these commandments I am giving you today. You must teach them to your children and talk about them when you are at home or out for a walk; at bedtime and the first thing in the morning. (Deut. 6:4-7, TLB)

O my people, listen to my teaching. Open your ears to what I am saying. For I will show you lessons from our history, stories handed down to us from former generations. I will reveal these truths to you so that you can describe these glorious deeds of Jehovah to your children, and tell them about the mighty miracles he did. For he gave his laws to Israel, and commanded our fathers to teach them to their children, so that they in turn could teach their children too. Thus his laws passed down from generation to generation. In this way each generation has been able to obey his laws and to set its hope anew on God and not forget his glorious miracles. (Ps. 78:1-7, TLB)

Reverence for God gives a man deep strength; his children have a place of refuge and security. (Prov. 14:26, TLB)

An old man's grandchildren are his crowning glory. A child's glory is his father. (Prov. 17:6, TLB)

Love forgets mistakes; nagging about them parts the best of friends. (Prov. 17:9, TLB)

Teach a child to choose the right path, and when he is older he will remain upon it. (Prov. 22:6, TLB)

And now a word to you parents. Don't keep on scolding and nagging your children, making them angry and resentful. Rather, bring them up with the loving discipline the Lord himself approves, with suggestions and godly advice. (Eph. 6:4, TLB)

"I Would Be There Alone."

Gerald Kennedy reports an interesting interview of a sociologist with some teen-agers "regarding their impressions of their homes and parents":

> Strangely enough he discovered that those who had been brought up permissively were not very appreciative of that experience, and those who had been disciplined were grateful for it. One girl told the interviewer that she lived in an apartment in a big city, and after supper in the summer the children on the block gathered in the streets to play. But after a while, one would say that she had to go home because her mother had told her to be in before eight o'clock. Or a father would whistle, and a boy would have to leave. A mother would call, and others would have to go. The girl said, "They would all go. It would get dark, and I would be there alone waiting for my father or my mother to call me in. They never did."[3]

Appendix B

Epilogue: God Calling

God Calling

Soon after I started to collect materials for this book, I picked up a little book called *God Calling: By Two Listeners*.[1]

For the benefit of any of you who may be unfamiliar with this book, let me just begin with a brief quotation from the Foreword by the editor:

> Not one woman, but two, have written this book; and they seek no praise. They have elected to remain anonymous and to be called "Two Listeners." But the claim which they make is an astonishing one, that their message has been given to them, today, here in England, by the Living Christ himself.
>
> Having read their book, I believe them.

In the first message "The Voice Divine," one of the listeners explains how she and a friend ("a deeply spiritual woman with unwavering faith in the goodness of God and a devout believer in prayer") decided to share a daily quiet time of prayer together to seek God's guidance. A very wonderful thing happened. She writes:

> From the first, beautiful messages were given ... by our Lord Himself, and every day from then on these messages have never failed us.

A little further on, she said something which caught my eye as I was thinking about *this* book which was beginning to take shape in my mind:

> Always, and this daily, He insisted that we should be channels of Love, Joy and Laughter in His broken world. This was the Man of Sorrows in a new light. To laugh, to cheer others, to be always joyful when days were pain-wracked, nights tortured by chronic insomnia, when poverty and almost insupportable worry were our daily

portion, when prayer went unanswered and God's face was veiled and fresh calamities came upon us?

Still comes this insistent command to love, and laugh, and be joy-bringers to the lives we contacted.

I reread that paragraph with mounting excitement. What a confirmation of my urgency to write about joy! With eager anticipation I turned the pages of *God Calling* and was not disappointed.

The book consists of messages, one for each day of the year, and of the 365 messages, more than fifty make references to the need for joy in the life of would-be followers of the Lord! Some of these are brief reminders, just a sentence. Others are a whole page or more. A number of them are based on Jesus' words to us in the gospels.

I had a strange, sure sense that I had not picked up the book by "accident" but that God himself had led me to it. Obviously space will not permit the inclusion of all these messages but a number are included below, and if you can accept them as genuine *"Words of Jesus—to You,"* your life cannot fail to be enriched thereby.

> Joy is the result of faithful, trusting acceptance of My Will, when it seems not joyous. (January 8)
>
> Joy is the whole being's attitude of "Thank You" to Me. Be glad. Rejoice. A father loves to see his children happy. (January 12)
>
> Be glad all the time. Rejoice exceedingly. Joy in Me. . . . "Underneath are the everlasting arms." (January 21)
>
> Man's ecstasy is God's touch on quickened, responsive spirit-nerves. Joy. Joy. Joy. (March 14)
>
> Life knows no greater joy than you will have in converse with Me. (March 17)

Laughter is the outward expression of Joy. That is why I urge upon you Love and Laughter. (March 30)

Joy—radiant Joy must be yours. Change all disappointment ... into Joy. Change each complaint into Joy. (April 22)

Radiate Joy. Not only must you rejoice, but your Joy must be made manifest.... Men must see and know your Joy, and seeing it, know without any doubt, that it springs from trust in Me, from living with Me. (November 21)

Live to bring others to Me, the only Source of Happiness and Heart peace. (December 30)

"If a man is unhappy," wrote Epictetus, a slave in Nero's Rome, "remember that his unhappiness is his own fault; for God made all men to be happy."

NOTES

Chapter 1

1. Definitions in the following paragraphs are from *The Random House Dictionary of the English Language* (New York: Random House, Inc., 1966).
2. Quoted in Gerald Kennedy's *Second Reader's Notebook* (New York: Harper & Brothers, 1959) No. 117.
3. *My God, Why?* Wallace Viets (Nashville, Tenn.: Abingdon Press), pp. 92-93.
4. *Selected Poems of John Oxenham* (New York: Harper & Brothers, 1948).
5. "The House Filled with Smoke," by T.M. Taylor. *University of Edinburgh Journal*, vol. xvi, no. 2, (1952), p. 86.
6. From "The Bridegroom of Beauty."
7. *New Life* by Andrew Murray, (Minneapolis, Minn.: Bethany Fellowship, Inc.), 1965.
8. *Fresh Every Morning* (New York: Harper & Row, 1966), p. 74.
9. *Altar Stairs* (New York: The Macmillan Company, 1938).

Chapter 2

1. *The Renewal of Man* (New York: Doubleday & Company, Inc., 1955).
2. *The Kingdom Here and Now* (Old Tappan, N.J.: Fleming H. Revell Co., 1976), pp. 184-185.
3. An Abbreviated Bible Commentary (Grand Rapids, Mich.: Zondervan Publishing House. Original © 1927), pp. 400-401.

⁴ By Roy and Revel Hession (Fort Washington, PA: Christian Literature Crusade, 1958), p. 26.

Chapter 3
1. *We Would See Jesus* by Roy and Revel Hession (Fort Washington, PA: Christian Literature Crusade, 1958), pp. 16-17.
2. *Guide to Understanding the Bible* by Harry Emerson Fosdick, (New York: Harper & Row, 1938), p. 63.
3. Edited by Madeleine S. Miller and J. Lane Miller (New York: Harper & Row Publishers, Inc., Eighth revised edition, 1973).
4. *Spiritual Letters of Father Congreve* (Milwaukee, Wisconsin: Morehouse).

Chapter 4
1. *The Second Reader's Notebook*, No. 1171.
2. *Invitation to Joy* by Lily M. Gyldenvand (Minneapolis, Minn.: Augsburg Publishing House, 1969), pp. 9-12, 14-15.
3. *The New Life* by Andrew Murray (Minneapolis, Minn.: Bethany Fellowship, Inc., 1965), pp. 140-141.
4. *For This Day* (Waco, Texas: Word Books, 1975), pp. 16-17.

Chapter 5
1. *The New Life* by Andrew Murray (Minneapolis, Minn.: Bethany Fellowship, Inc., 1965), pp. 155-156.

Chapter 7
1. *New Every Morning* (New York: Harper & Row, 1966), p. 45.

2. *The Meaning of Service* (New York: Association Press, 1920).
3. *Instrument of Thy Peace* (New York: Seabury Press, 1968), p. 28.
4. Ibid., pp. 11-12.
5. *A Testament of Devotion* (Living Selections from the Great Devotional Classics). Arranged and edited by Douglas V. Steere. (Nashville, Tenn.: The Upper Room. Copyright by Harper & Brothers.)
6. E.M. Blandy in *Hymns of Glorious Praise* (Springfield, Missouri: Gospel Publishing House, 1969), No. 372.
7. *A Twentieth Century Testimony* (Thomas Nelson, Inc., 1978).
8. *The Kingdom Here and Now* (Old Tappan, New Jersey: Fleming H. Revell, 1976), p.185.
9. George Matheson (1842-1906).

Chapter 8
1. *Journey into Joy* (Madras, India: The Christian Literature Society and the Indian Society for Promoting Christian Knowledge, Delhi, 1972. American edition: William B. Eerdmans Publishing Company, Grand Rapids, Michigan.)
2. Ibid., pp. 112-113.
3. *The Christian's Secret of a Happy Life* (Old Tappan, New Jersey: Fleming H. Revell Company, MCMLII), p. 200.
4. *Those Who Love Him* (Grand Rapids, Michigan: Zondervan Publishing House), pp. 12-13.
5. *Hymns of Glorious Praise* (Springfield, Missouri: Gospel Publishing House, 1969), No. 358.

6. From "The Celestial Surgeon" in *Ballads and Other Poems* by Robert Louis Stevenson. (New York: Charles Scribner's Sons, 1895).

Chapter 9
1. Dr. Howard Bliss, who shortly after this succeeded his father (and, I believe, his grandfather) as president of the American University at Beirut.
2. *Collected Verse of Edgar A. Guest* (Chicago, Ill.: Reilly & Lee Co., 1934).

Chapter 10
1. Title of an article in *The Christian Herald*, February, 1979, by Dr. Calvin D. Linton.
2. By the Rev. J. Willard Jarvis, pastor of The Redeemer's Church, Columbus, Ohio.

Chapter 11
1. *The Christian's Secret of a Happy Life* by Hannah Whitall Smith. (Old Tappan, New Jersey: Fleming H. Revell Company MCMLII), p. 78.
2. (Waco, Texas: Word Books, 1975), p. 168.
3. *From Everlasting to Everlasting* by Florence Taylor (New York: The Seabury Press, 1973), pp. 140-141.
4. A Bantam Book, published by arrangement with Harper & Row. Bantam edition, 1972.
5. Ibid., p. 168.
6. Ibid., p. 169.
7. Ibid., p. 174.
8. Ibid.
9. *Collected Poems of Ella Wheeler Wilcox* (Chicago: Rand McNally & Co., Conkey Division).

10 *The Hiding Place*, (Lincoln, Virginia: Chosen Books, 1971), pp. 179-181.
11 Ibid., pp. 189-190.
12 *The Mystery of Pain* by Paul J. Linden (Minneapolis, Minn.: Augsburg Publishing House, 1974), p. 59.
13 Samuel Rodigast, c. 1674. Tr. by Catherine Winkworth, 1858.

Chapter 12

1 *A Table in the Wilderness.* Tyndale House, 1965.
2 *Living Creatively* by Kirby Page (New York: Farrar & Rinehart, 1932), p. 70.
3 William W. How, 1823-1897.
4 (New York: Harper & Row, 1966), pp. 61-60.

Chapter 13

1 *The Cheerful Cherub* by Rebecca McCann (New York: Covici Friede, 1932), p. 21.
2 Ibid., p. 423.
3 *The New Life* (Minneapolis, Minn.: Bethany Fellowship, Inc., 1965), p. 157.
4 *Thou Didst Open Up My Life: Selections from the Rufus Jones Collection*, edited by Mary Hoxie Jones. (Wallingford, PA: Pendle Hill Pamphlet No. 127, 1963), p. 11.
5 (New York: Harper & Row, 1966), p. 216.
6 Johnson Oatman, Jr. 1858-1922.
7 From *The Book of Common Prayer* according to the use of the Protestant Episcopal Church.

Chapter 14

1. From *From Everlasting to Everlasting*, by Florence M. Taylor (New York: The Seabury Press, 1973), pp. 77-79. Altered.
2. *Guesses at the Truth*, 1827.
3. pp. 199-224.

Chapter 15

1. *The Way to Power and Praise* (Nashville: Abingdon-Cokesbury Press, MCMXLIX), p. 233.
2. Ibid., p. 234.
3. Ibid., p. 235.
4. Ibid., p. 239.
5. *Personal Religion and the Life of Fellowship* (1946), p. 46.
6. (Lincoln, Virginia: Chosen Books, 1971), pp. 214-215.

Chapter 16

1. *In The Morning, Bread* by Florence M. Taylor (New Canaan, Conn.: Keats Publishing Company, 1976), Day 179.
2. Ibid., Day 180.
3. *A Simple Method of Raising the Soul to Contemplation* (1669). English translation, 1931. Pp. 80f.
4. (Notre Dame, Indiana: Ave Maria Press, 1975), pp. 20-24.
5. In *Prayers for Services*, by Morgan P. Noyes (New York: Charles Scribner's Sons, 1934), p. 111.

Chapter 17

[1] In *For This Day* by J.B. Phillips (Waco, Texas: Word Books, 1975), pp. 89-90.

[2] From *To Die Is Gain* by Neal Carlson (Grand Rapids, Michigan: Baker Book House, 1974).

[3] *How to Get Through Your Struggles* by Oral Roberts. (Tulsa, Oklahoma), pp. 24-25.

[4] *Selections from the Writings of William Temple*, arranged and edited by Sulon G. Ferre. (Great Devotional Classics, Nashville, Tenn.; The Upper Room, 1968), pp. 24-25.

Chapter 18

[1] *In The Morning, Bread* by Florence M. Taylor (New Canaan, Conn.: Keats Publishing, Inc., 1976), Day 45.

[2] *The Imitation of Christ* by Thomas a Kempis.

[3] *Selections from the Writings of Soren Kierkegaard*, pp. 16-17. Altered.

[4] *Selections from the Writings of John Bunyan*, p. 40. Altered.

[5] Ibid., p. 20. Altered.

[6] *The Life of God in the Soul of Man* by Henry Sconpal, p. 25.

[7] Paul Lambourne Higgins.

[8] *Selections from the Journal of John Wesley*. Altered.

[9] In *Seed Grains of Prayer*, (Columbus, Ohio: The Hartburg Press, n.d.).

[10] Source unknown.

[11] William E. Channing, in *God of a Hundred Names*, Barbara Greene and Kern Gollancz. Altered.

12. Lucy Helen Muriel Soulsby in *An Anthology of Prayers*, ed. by A.S.T. Fisher. Altered.
13. Francis G. Peabody in *Prayers for Services* by Morgan Phelps Noyes. (New York: Charles Scribner's Sons, 1934), p. 101.
14. William Adams Brown in *The Quiet Hour*. Altered.
15. Thomas Trahern, in *God of a Hundred Names*, p.258.
16. Henry Martyn, in *God of a Hundred Names*, p. 34.
17. Walter Rauschenbush, in *Prayers of the Social Awakening*.
18. Benjamin Jenks. Altered.
19. John Baillie in *A Diary of Private Prayer* (New York: Charles Schribner's Sons, 1949), p. 91.
20. In *The Book of Common Worship* (Presbyterian: 1946). Altered.
21. Phillips Brooks, in *A Pocket Prayerbook and Devotional Guide*, compiled by Ralph Spaulding Cushman (Nashville: The Upper Room, 1941), p. 52. Altered.
22. George Matheson, in *The Meaning of Prayer*, Harry Emerson Fosdick (Boston: The Pilgrim Press, 1915), p. 25.
23. John Baillie, in *A Diary of Private Prayer*.
24. In *God of a Hundred Names*, p. 259.
25. In *Seed Grains of Prayer*. (Columbus, Ohio: The Hartburg Press, n.d.), p. 345.
26. Charles Wesley.
27. Jay T. Stocking.
28. Attributed to Bernard of Clairvaux.
29. Henry Van Dyke.
30. Washington Gladden.

Appendix A
[1] Sir Thomas Buxton, in *I Quote*, Virginia Ely.
[2] *The Art of Loving*, (New York: Harper & Row, 1956), pp. 41-42.
[3] *Fresh Every Morning*, (New York: Harper & Row, 1966), p. 30.

Appendix B
[1] Edited by A.J. Russell. (Old Tappan, New Jersey: Fleming H. Revell Company, Spire edition, 1972).

Acknowledgments

The author gratefully acknowledges her use of the following sources in her preparation of *That Your Joy May Be Full:*

Journey into Joy by Leslie Newbigin. Reprinted by permission of William B. Eerdmans Publishing Co.

Scripture quotations from the New American Standard Bible © The Lockman Foundation 1960, 1962, 1963, 1968, 1971, 1972, 1973, 1975, 1977.

"God hath not Promised" by Annie Johnson Flint. Reprint. Permission granted, Evangelical Publishers, Toronto, Canada.

Material from *Halley's Bible Handbook*, copyright © 1965 by Halley's Bible Handbook, Inc. Reprinted by permission.

"The Gospel According to Job," by Dr. Calvin D. Linton. *The Christian Herald*, February, 1979. Excerpts used by permission.

The New Testament in Modern English, Revised Edition, J.B. Phillips, translator. Copyright © J.B. Phillips, 1958, 1960, 1972.

Scripture quotations designated GNB are from the *Good News Bible*, the Bible in Today's English Version. Copyright © American Bible Society, 1976. Used with permission.

Verses marked TLB are taken from *The Living Bible*, copyright © 1971 by Tyndale House Publishers, Wheaton, IL. Used by permission.

The Hebrew Morning Service is taken from the Authorized Daily Prayer Book of the United Hebrew Congregations of the British Empire (trans. Rev. S. Singer). Copyright Singer Prayer Book Publication Committee.

The Kingdom Here and Now by Malcolm Smith. Old Tappan, NJ: Fleming H. Revell Publishing Co., 1976. Used with permission.

"The House Filled with Smoke," by T.M. Taylor, *University of Edinburgh Journal*, vol. xvi, no. 2 (1952). Used with permission of the University of Edinburgh.

Excerpts from *Poustinia* by Catherine de Hueck Doherty. Copyright © 1975 by Ave Maria Press, Notre Dame, IN 46556. Used with permission of the publisher.

Excerpts from *The Mystery of Pain* by Paul Lindell, copyright © Augsburg Publishing House. Reprinted by permission.

Excerpts from *Invitation to Joy* by Lily M. Gyldenvand, copyright © 1969 Augsburg Publishing House. Reprinted by permission.

Excerpts from *How to Get Through Your Struggles* by Oral Roberts, used with permission.

Excerpts from *The Hiding Place*, copyright © 1971, by Corrie ten Boom and John and Elizabeth Sherrill. Published by Chosen Books, Lincoln, VA 22078. Used by permission.

Excerpts from *A Table in the Wilderness* by Watchman Nee. Published by Tyndale House Publishers, Inc., copyright © 1965 by Angus I. Kinnear. Used by permission.

Excerpt from *The Modern Language Bible: The Berkeley Version in Modern English* copyright © 1945, 1959, 1969 by Zondervan Publishing House. Used by permission.

Excerpts from *The Christian's Secret of a Happy Life* by Hannah Whitall Smith. Used with permission of Fleming H. Revell Co.

Excerpts from *My God, Why?* by Wallace Vietz and *The Way to Power and Poise* by E. Stanley Jones, reprinted with permission of Abingdon Press.

Excerpts from *To Die Is Gain* by Neal Carson. Copyright © 1974 by Baker Book House and used by permission.

Excerpts from *The New Life* by Andrew Murray, published and copyright © 1965 Bethany House Publishers, Minneapolis, MN 55438. Used with permission.

Excerpt from *The Renewal of Man* by Alexander Miller. Copyright © 1955 by Alexander Miller. Reprinted by permission of Doubleday and Company, Inc.

Excerpts from *A Twentieth Century Testimony* by Malcolm Muggeridge. Copyright © 1978 by Evangelische Omroep. Reprinted by permission of Thomas Nelson, Inc., Publishers.

Excerpts from *Thou Dost Open Up My Life: Selections from the Rufus Jones Collection,* reprinted by permission of Pendle Hill Publications.

Excerpts from *Instrument of Thy Peace* by Alan Paton, copyright © 1968 by The Seabury Press, Inc. Used by permission.